RINGSIDE

*My Life Outside the Ropes
and the Octagon*

■ ■ ■

By
Marc Ratner

Copyright © 2021 By Marc Ratner

All rights reserved. This book or any portion thereof may not be reproduced or used in any manner whatsoever without the express written permission of the publisher except for the use of brief quotations in a book review.

To my wife Jody, and my children and grandchildren who inspired me to write this book.

To Lorenzo Fertitta, Dana White, Lawrence Epstein, Sig Rogich, and Dr. James Nave, my mentors, whose wisdom and friendship I will forever cherish and be thankful for.

To Matt Cohn and Andrew Schleimer, who shepherded the idea through the various UFC departments to have this published.

To those who made special contributions to this book, including Heidi Noland, Rob Tonelete, Julie Tran, Jeff Bottari, Rachel Greene, and the countless others who have impacted me and my career along the way.

Thank you.

Table of Contents

■ ■ ■

Chapter One	Dressing Room Walls	1
Chapter Two	A Kid at the Dawn of Vegas	9
Chapter Three	The Enforcer	21
Chapter Four	Eyes on the Corner	30
Chapter Five	Hands on the Canvas	38
Chapter Six	Iron Age	50
Chapter Seven	Tyson's Return and 'Bite Night'	56
Chapter Eight	The Bizarre and the Tragic	69
Chapter Nine	Money and Mayhem	76
Chapter Ten	Joining the Fight	90
Chapter Eleven	The Quest for 50	102
Chapter Twelve	Fight Week	112
Chapter Thirteen	Notorious	130
Epilogue		139
End Notes		143

CHAPTER ONE

■ ■ ■

Dressing Room Walls

"The sweet science is joined onto the past like man's arm to his shoulder."
—A.J. Liebling[1]

August 2016

Inside the walls of a dressing room, the fight to come always reveals itself. If you know what to look and listen for, those dressing rooms tell you so much. When you've seen as many as I have, you know how to take it all in. During my 35-year career in the fighting world, I've been in all kinds—loud and boisterous, quiet and composed, silent and eerie, casual in a good way, casual in a troubling way.

In combat sports, where it's just two people facing off with nothing between them, how the fighters act in the dressing room beforehand speaks volumes: about their preparation, their mindset, their confidence, and their attitude—about what's going to happen in the ring and who is going to be standing when it's all over.

If those walls could talk, the gamblers would have a field day.

I'm a regulator. That's what I do. I make sure the rules are being followed so the fight can go on. So that it's fair. So that the fighters, their camps, the fans, companies, media, gamblers, and spectators can trust it. Otherwise, it's anarchy. Both boxing and mixed martial arts (MMA) certainly can be brutal, but the whole thing is bound together by rules. They're written and enforced by the names you don't know and the faces you won't see.

That's where I come in.

On the night of August 26, 2017, I found myself inside Dressing Room 7 at T-Mobile Arena in Las Vegas before what was being billed as the "Fight of the Century." In a sport known for its hype and hyperbole, this time it might've actually been true. It was the meeting of the two biggest stars of their respective sports: UFC champion Conor McGregor was stepping into the boxing ring against undefeated welterweight champion Floyd Mayweather, Jr. The fight was one of the most covered and touted sports events of my lifetime—of anyone's lifetime. And just outside the center, in a spot where no one would notice me, there I was. It's where I like to be. I've always been comfortable there.

Floyd was 40 years old, coming out of retirement for a one-off match-up. He was a resident, prodigal son, and a beloved staple of Las Vegas, his image painted on a 200-foot mural down the side of MGM Grand. He had come to embody Las Vegas with his shine and confidence. McGregor, who I'd known since his UFC debut in 2013, was an Irish MMA fighter with a thick accent, a whole lot of braggadocio, and more than enough chops to back it up. He was one of UFC's biggest stars, and the hype around the fight was as elevated as anything I'd ever seen. In our business, the hype is just part and parcel of the deal.

The Tuesday before the event, I was at my UFC headquarters office when I ran into Audie Attar, Conor's manager. Conor had been training just about every day at the UFC Performance Institute, in another wing of the headquarters, sparring and relearning the basics of boxing, which he had dabbled in before going into MMA. A fight is not just a fight—and Conor had to figure out how to adapt to this new sport, in which he was expected to take on an undefeated champion.

I had to hand it to him. He believed in himself as much as anyone I'd ever seen.

"Hey Marc," Audie said, popping his head into my office. Audie had slicked-back hair and the broad shoulders of a linebacker, which he once was at UCLA. "Listen, I was wondering if you could do us a favor since Floyd knows you. We'd like you to watch him get his hands wrapped Saturday night…if that's alright with you."

"Sure thing," I said. "I'll be there. I don't have any major duties. Happy to do it." I don't know if Audie knew that's how I got started in this business—watching fighters wrap their hands—but he felt I'd be the right emissary for it.

Tension was high between both sides, especially after an international press tour on which Floyd, Conor, and their respective camps traveled for four straight days to Los Angeles, Toronto, New York, and London to promote the fight. "Press conference" is a generous term, as those events were loud and intense, with the fighters getting right up in each other's faces exchanging colorful language about what they were going to do to each other. Conor wanted me to be his eyes inside Floyd's dressing room, to make sure everything was on the up-and-up.

A lot was riding on the fight—for everyone. With that anticipation and tension came some suspicion. So, they turned to me. My career straddled both sports, and in both worlds, I was known as a rules guy. Maybe I was a natural choice to play ambassador between the two sides. After 14 years running the Nevada State Athletic Commission, in many ways the governing body of professional boxing, I was now an executive with UFC—the Vice President of Regulatory Affairs. Because Mayweather-McGregor was a boxing match, I had no official role that night. I was there as a representative of Conor's camp and as a fan. And, now, I'd be a witness to what the other guy was up to. Conor and his people trusted me, but they also knew Floyd's camp would be okay with me in there, watching his hands get wrapped. The last thing anyone wanted was a fight before the actual fight. I've seen those before; those dressing rooms can get pretty contentious.

The wrong person in there, hovering over the wrapping and voicing protests, would be like a lit match thrown on gasoline.

Floyd and I had known each other for more than 20 years, since he was a 19-year-old amateur who had just turned pro. I was at his very first fight against a journeyman named Roberto Apodaca, present as the director of the Nevada State Athletic Commission. It was a few months after Floyd medaled in the 1996 Olympics, and his fight was quite a way down the card. It was at a hotel-casino named Texas Station, located off the Las Vegas Strip on the western part of town.

That venue was decidedly less glamorous than T-Mobile Arena: movable bleachers on four sides, a big television in the corner, the dressing rooms curtained off inside the hotel's ballroom. Most of the fights are like that, not garnering a Pay-Per-View audience or cable coverage. That's where guys earn their stripes, work out their kinks, and get the reps necessary to develop a professional career. Floyd had a baby face in those days (and even a little bit of hair), but he already showed flashes of what would make him among the greatest—a tough chin and a fluid movement that made it near impossible to hit him square. Back then his moniker was "Pretty Boy," after the famous bank robber. But nowadays, he goes by "Money." That's what all his people call him. But I still call him Floyd, or sometimes, Champ.

I entered Floyd's dressing room on the night of Mayweather-McGregor. It was filled with security people, some friends and family, media members, and various people on "The Money Team." The room was nice and expansive, almost like a lounge: mirrors, carpet, and leather chairs with the sound of casual conversation and an undercurrent of music. I've been in tight and tense dressing rooms in my life, but this one was smooth. It was not a party exactly, but it certainly had a leisurely vibe. The atmosphere takes its cue from the fighter.

Sure enough, I found Floyd, relaxed and confident wearing a white tank top, sitting in a chair. A masseuse was rubbing his shoulders and arms, getting him loose while he talked to Leonard Ellerbe, his manager. Leonard, the CEO of Mayweather Promotions, had a big round head, flashy sunglasses, and neatly trimmed goatee. I shook hands and said hello to Leonard and Al Haymon, Floyd's advisor—an older and quieter gentleman who liked to keep out of the public eye. I think he watched the fight that night from the dressing room. Floyd's trainer, his father, and some of his children were there, too. A television camera was positioned right at Floyd documenting everything, as it had been doing all week. Floyd didn't seem too concerned about the match—not as much as he would be against another fighter. After all, his opponent wasn't even a boxer.

"Hey, Champ. Good to see you," I said. "How you doing?" He reached out for my hand, and we exchanged some brief pleasantries. Some fighters are hard, a bit guarded. It takes time to earn their trust because I'm a "government" guy, a regulator, one of the suits. There's always a little distance because I can't exactly be their friend or go to lunch with them, but I always love talking to them, especially the greats. Boxing is one of the sports where the greats just loom larger, in style, in aura and in the energy they bring into a room.

I took a spot next to the inspector for the Nevada State Athletic Commission, who had Floyd's gloves dangling around his neck. Floyd's team operated like a well-tuned machine, which was obvious by the routine I witnessed. His outfit was laid out carefully, and after he put his shorts on, he laced on his boxing shoes himself. It was all very deliberate and meticulous. That's the way he liked it, and since he had never lost, he didn't want to change the routine. It was likely a mix of superstition and preparation.

Bob Ware, a veteran corner guy, took a seat in front of Floyd and began wrapping the gauze around the champ's hands and then his knuckles. Ware is an institution in and of himself—part of boxing history. One thing I love about the sport is that continuous through line that runs inside all of it: the trainers who are a direct link back to the old days, whose stories can put you right there with Sonny Liston or Sugar Ray Robinson or Ali; the fighters, who—through wins, losses, titles, and retirements—you can trace all the way back to Joe Louis and Jack Dempsey and Rocky Marciano. There's not just tradition and history, but lineage. It's what makes the sport so galvanizing.

A boxer's hands are his livelihood, so a lot of trust is put into the process. It's just gauze, tape, and scissors, but there's an art to it. Floyd had brittle hands throughout his career, so he was very particular about his wraps. Floyd watched the process closely, at one point asking Ware to do one part again. As he finished, he cut the gauze, and I started to get that feeling in my stomach that comes on fight night.

I've always loved the anticipation of those big fights, the matches that you knew were going to be a part of history before the first bell even rang. Twenty thousand people were waiting outside those walls and millions more from their homes all over the world, but Floyd was completely cool. It starts at the fighter and moves all the way down. How the fighter goes, his people go, the room goes, and the fight goes.

■ ■ ■

When the idea first started to get kicked around—for Conor to fight Floyd—my initial reaction was that of a regulator, someone who was responsible for licensing fighters and approving fights, which I did in Nevada for much of my career. *How are we going to approve this?* I thought. *McGregor has never had a pro fight, but we're going to give him a debut against the champ who is undefeated and one of the best fighters in the world?* Let everyone else talk about ratings and money and history. My concern was fundamental: Can we even do this?

As I usually do in those situations, I looked to history to find precedent, something we could hang our hat on. My first thought was of a different Floyd, heavyweight champion Floyd Patterson. In 1957, Patterson fought Pete Rademacher, who turned pro after winning a gold medal at the previous year's Olympics. Incredibly, his pro debut was for the heavyweight championship of the world, the only time that had ever happened. ("The worst mismatch in boxing history," Joe Louis called it). Rademacher actually managed to get Patterson on the canvas once, but Floyd knocked him down seven times and won handily in the sixth round.

So, it had happened before, 60 years ago and only once, but still. That mattered to me.

There's the glory, the hype, the media, and the presentation, but for sports to work—*especially* combat sports—there needs to be precedent and structure and rules or else it would all go off the rails. Rules are not as glamorous as a stare-down or a knockout, but it's as much a part of the sport as anything. The rules underpin everything else. It's the steady bass note that makes the rest of the song work. In a sport where people are suspicious and at each other's throats, sometimes literally, I became one of the trustworthy ones. My career was built on that reputation.

Mayweather-McGregor was a big deal for sports, and the culture at large, but it was also personal for me. The fight represented a culmination of my career up to that point, the merging of my two worlds, the marriage of my past and future. Boxing was my older child who had grown up and left home, and MMA was my new child who I was still raising. There's no reason I couldn't feel affection for them both. And just like a parent of a younger child, it was important to me that MMA be taken seriously. I didn't want Floyd to embarrass our guy. (Fortunately, our guy wasn't easily embarrassed.) But still, no one knew what was going to happen inside those ropes.

For the fight, Floyd was coming out of retirement. He had an undefeated record and the chance to beat Rocky Marciano's legendary 49-0. Conor was game for it, maybe in order to legitimize himself as a fighter, maybe as a chance to elevate MMA, or maybe because he sought a shot at being considered the best. Of course, there was some protest, mostly from the old guard who thought the idea of a boxer going up against an MMA fighter was wrong. It *shouldn't* happen, the traditionalists said. There were those who were never going to give MMA legitimacy like that, and maybe they were afraid Conor would win. Then where would they be?

The thing that raised the anticipation even higher than

previous contests, even the biggest title fights, was the novelty of it, the unprecedented nature of it. A first-round knockout by Floyd would've validated all the people who were against it happening in the first place. There was also some concern as to whether or not Conor would revert to something in MMA. If he was in trouble, would he unconsciously throw a knee? Plus, none of his corner guys had ever been in a boxing corner, so I imagine the inspectors were extra vigilant. I thought about Johnny Tocco—dead for 20 years, who taught just about every inspector, including me, all the basics. I wondered what he would've thought of all this. He loved a good fight as much as anyone, so I imagine he'd have been up for it.

They were writing a new chapter in combat sports history that night, and it was electric. It felt new, but it also felt old—part of a long tradition. Every fight was connected to the previous fight, in this expanding line that ran through history, through the record books and through my own mind. I kept the ticket stubs to all of them and have flash memories of most. Boxing is fascinating because the fights are all birthed from the previous fights—who's up for fighting who, who's ready for a shot at the title, who gets the rematch. It has its own history, and I've been fortunate to be part of it.

I started as just a kid who loved going to the fights. Las Vegas never had a professional sports team: boxing, especially in the rotunda at the old Convention Center, was all there was, and the big fighters came through Las Vegas. Plus, it was accessible—you could get up close. In a million years, I never could have guessed where I'd end up. If you told me back then that I'd one day be in those dressing rooms talking to the fighters, in front of the scale weighing them, sitting ringside or standing on the apron watching the corners or talking to the referee, I wouldn't have believed you. You might as well have told me I'd be going to Mars.

CHAPTER TWO

■ ■ ■

A Kid at the Dawn of Vegas

"The thrill of heavyweights is in the way they punch. The blows come in slow motion in comparison to those of smaller fighters. Fans in the nosebleed seats can follow their arc. And they land hard."
—Thomas Hauser[2]

In 1956, the summer before I started eighth grade, my family moved from Pomona, California to Las Vegas. At the time I arrived, I was 12 years old, and it was like the city was also in its adolescence. It had been about a decade since the famous mobster Bugsy Siegel built his Flamingo Hotel and Casino in the middle of nowhere, but the city was not yet the mecca of gambling and glitz it would become. But clearly the place was on the verge of something. Even a boy could tell. There were fewer than 60,000 people (compared to 2 million today) and only a few hotels on what became the Las Vegas Strip. Looking back, it was as though the city itself was rising out of the ground.

It was hard for me to pick up and move to a new and strange place, having to make friends all over again. But I was a lucky kid, given a ringside seat to Las Vegas' rise, its bloom into the fight and entertainment capital of the world. I remember looking out the class window in eighth grade to see a huge truck carrying the one-day iconic sign for the Stardust Hotel, which hadn't even opened yet. That image of it, shiny and new on the back of a flatbed truck, encapsulates what that era was like. Everything was just being born.

We didn't live that far from the Strip, and my friends and I would ride our bikes up and down it, dropping into the early hotel casinos like the El Rancho and the Sands to get souvenirs. We'd walk up to the cashiers and ask for postcards or dice or chips (they punch holes in those before giving them us, so we couldn't use them). Decades later, it's hard to imagine kids wandering into casinos—for freebies, no less—but back then, it was common. It was a less exclusive world, and the walls hadn't been erected separating the locals from the tourists from the celebrities from the big spenders.

We were all mixed together in this strange, beautiful place that didn't quite know what it was yet. It was like the world's flashiest small town. Past the Hacienda, the last hotel, there was a small airport with only a handful of gates. The city was an undiscovered place, a secret to those who knew about it, reserved for the locals, the adventurous, and the famous. When I close my eyes, I can still picture all of it. It comes through in this gauzy, almost sepia-toned string of images.

■ ■ ■

What brought my family to Las Vegas was my father's business, Ace-Hy Beauty Supply. He opened a store that sold hair dryers, hydraulic beauty and barber chairs, and other supplies to salons and barbershops around town. As a teenager, after school and on weekends, I worked in the store and made deliveries to places like the new Caesars Palace or the Sands. I still remember the day I delivered a hair dryer to Ann-Margret on the film set of "Viva Las Vegas." When I was let into her room at the Sands, I saw Elvis Presley on a chair and her on the bed, both with scripts in hand. Years later, I saw the King perform many times at the Las Vegas Hilton, and he was incapable of disappointing. When he sang a ballad, he'd slowly take off his scarves and hand them out to adoring female fans who were like soft putty in his hands. Back then, he was just the epitome of young and cool.

Other celebrities made their way through town, some more furtive than others. In May 1959, I was going through my confirmation classes at our synagogue, Temple Beth Shalom, when we were told one day we couldn't use the regular sanctuary because of a private event. Later, we saw this couple sneaking out the back: Elizabeth Taylor and Eddie Fisher. They had just gotten married in secret, an event which made news all over the country once it was uncovered. I probably could've sold the info to a gossip rag if I had known whom to call.

Living in Las Vegas gave us a chance see some big names at their peak or on the verge of their stardom: Harry Belafonte at a dinner show at the Riviera and a Liberace concert where the opening act was a young Barbra Streisand. She brought the house down with a version of "Cry Me A River" that left the crowd dumbstruck. I don't remember if she even had a microphone, but her voice came through crystal clear.

When the Beatles came to Las Vegas during their first U.S. tour in 1964, I saw them at the old Convention Center. I say that I "saw" them because I couldn't really hear a note—not over the sounds of all the girls shrieking. On TV, they show clips to this day of what they called "Beatlemania," but it doesn't come close to capturing what it was like being there in an auditorium among those screams bouncing off the walls, drowning out the sounds of microphones, electric guitars, and drums. I couldn't tell one song from the next, but I remember it all better than the lunch I had yesterday. That kind of thing never gets booted out of the memory bank.

My family would sometimes go to a dinner show at the Sands called "Starlight, Starbright," and you never knew who was going to show up. Often, it was some of the Rat Pack, who were carving out Las Vegas as their personal playground: Frank Sinatra, Dean Martin, Sammy Davis Jr., Joey Bishop, and Peter Lawford. You'd spot them around town and then read about their exploits in the paper. I spent my free time as a teenager wandering on the burgeoning Strip, which still had a good deal of empty spaces in between. It was smaller, more intimate, like the future was waiting to show up.

But, my favorite thing to do was to go to the fights. Boxing is synonymous with Las Vegas, and its history there goes way back. At the time, New York City was the mecca of the boxing world, but in the 1960s, Las Vegas began developing a reputation as "Fight City." I had gotten into boxing at exactly the right time and place. People don't realize the boxing history that exists in Nevada, where it has been legal since 1897, going back to the time of old mines. The famous Jack Johnson-Jim Jeffries title fight on July 4, 1910 took place in a wooden building in Reno in front of 20,000 spectators, almost double the city's population. It also "produced boxing's first full-fledged media circus," triggering more than a million Western Union messages, a record at the time.[3] Celebrities from all over came to town, and for that one night, Nevada was the center of the sports world. It would take decades, but the sport would return to the desert.

Throughout its heyday in the 1940s and 1950s, boxing was centered in New York City, with the famed Madison Square Garden operating as ground zero of the fight world. In the late 1950s, when television began to cut into the profits for local fights, government investigators started poking around and uncovering mob and corruption scandals. In the words of one writer, New York had "broken the sport and sucked all the meat from its bones."[4] At the same time, the hotel-casinos spurted up in Las Vegas, in a city where gambling was legal, so boxing did as so many other Americans did and moved west. Fight packages became part of weekend entertainment once the casinos learned the fight crowd was also a gambling crowd. Another thing in Las Vegas' favor for hosting is that a fight had to be blacked out on local television until the event was sold out. In the (then) small city of Las Vegas, this result wouldn't hurt the broadcast companies the same way it would if they'd had to blackout fights in big cities like New York or Chicago.

The first fight I saw was with my father. It was outdoors at Cashman Field, sometime in the late 1950s. It was a less-than-ideal venue, with raised bleachers only on one side and the fighters in a ring placed on the infield dirt of a baseball field. It was probably an unimpressive spectacle to any veteran fight fan, but it was like I had fallen in love. I couldn't get enough of it. "Boxing is a story without words," Joyce Carol Oates wrote. I love that line. So much happens in inside those ropes: glory and defeat and drama and suspense and hope and despair. A good fight has a little bit of everything.

When I was old enough to drive, I'd go alone or with friends to a casino called the Silver Slipper that had fights every Wednesday night. It had an old western saloon setup on the first floor with live music and burlesque shows, though I never went to those. I'd always head upstairs, where one night a week, a boxing ring was set up in the ballroom. A few hundred people would crowd around to watch a rotating array of four and six round fights capped off by a 10-round main event. Along the room-length bar on the far wall, there was always lots of man-to-man betting, money being waved around and passing hands in that smoke-filled room.

At the Silver Slipper, I could get up really close, close enough to see the fighters' eyes. Most of the match-ups there were between new guys on their way up or once-wases on their way down. I'd catch them right before (or right after) they were somebody. I didn't care. It wasn't about the big names. I just loved watching two guys lace up their gloves and go toe-to-toe. As far as I was concerned, anyone who got in the ring was worth seeing. I always enjoyed the smaller fights, but over time, I was drawn to the big timers. Heavyweights brought a personality and shine to their fights. They carried an aura about them that lifted the stakes and injected more drama into the event.

One more than any other.

"It's just a job. Grass grows, birds fly, waves pound the sand. I beat people up."

—*Muhammad Ali*

The first time I saw Muhammad Ali, that wasn't even his name yet. The 19-year-old Olympic medalist already had strut and confidence. In June 1961, I was a high school sophomore in the crowd to see Cassius Clay take on a gigantic Hawaiian named Duke Sabedong, who had about 30 pounds and a six-inch advantage on him. The fight was at the old Convention Center, underneath the big silver dome that looked like a flying saucer. I was among the 2,500 people watching Clay's seventh professional fight, and it was clear this guy had something. At the end of each round, Duke would yell and pound on his chest, but no one was fooled. Duke lost every round, even resorting to low punches and other dirty tricks. He couldn't lay a hand on Clay, who always kept moving in what they would later call the "Ali Shuffle." Ali had not yet fully developed his speed and power. Boxing writer A.J. Liebling noted his "skittering style, like a pebble skittering over water."[5] But he was on his way.

The fight was actually a part of history, though I didn't know it at the time. During that week, while doing local press alongside wrestler Gorgeous George (who was in town to fight Freddie Blassie), Clay was inspired by George's brash persona, all-braggadocio and salesmanship. After taking in the match to witness George first-hand, Clay dropped in on the wrestler's dressing room where the two had a chat. "A lot of people will pay to see someone shut your mouth…" George told him. "Always be outrageous."[6] From then on, Clay made the George persona so much his own, jawing with the crowd and taunting his opponents, that the behavior forever became synonymous with Ali.[7] That's when the rhymes started, the playful back-and-forth with reporters, and his lofty claims of superior skills. Like many people, Clay came to Las Vegas and reinvented himself, becoming one of the greatest self-salesmen of all time. After the Sabedong fight was the first time Clay called himself "The Greatest"—a moniker he holds to this day. At the time, people just assumed he had a big mouth.

The next year, when I was a high school junior, my friend Sig Rogich and I went to our first title fight: Joe Brown-Carlos Ortiz for the lightweight championship. Former heavyweight champ Joe Louis, a Las Vegas fixture by that point, was also there, waving from the ring wearing a suit and bowtie. He was years into retirement then, and a professional greeter at Las Vegas hotels, but it was still something to have living history there in the building. The fighters were evenly matched in almost every physical way except that Brown was a full decade older. Ortiz took the title, and somehow after the fight, Sig and I were able to sneak into his dressing room. There were hordes of media and hangers-on and fans around (this was in the years before tight security), and we noticed his two horsehair gloves sitting on a table. We each grabbed one and took off. I held onto that glove for years.

Before big concerts, there'd be lines out on the sidewalk, so I assumed the same held true for big prizefights. In 1963, I read in the newspaper that tickets for the second Liston versus Patterson fight were going on sale at 8 a.m. It was a heavily publicized rematch from a fight the previous September where Liston took Patterson's title after knocking him out in 126 seconds ("old-fashioned murder," one sportswriter called it.[8]) I set my alarm and got up with the sun, showing up outside the Convention Center the morning tickets went on sale. To my surprise, I found I was the only one on the sidewalk, for a good hour. When the box office opened, I proudly bought the first four tickets for $10 each for seats in the top row of the rotunda.

Back then, fighters would train every day at the same time, and for a dollar, anyone from the public could just show up and watch. Sonny Liston trained up on a stage in the showroom at the Thunderbird Hotel, so I drove down there that week to take a look. He was not a beloved fighter, not even well liked. He had this serious and almost frightening scowl permanently plastered on his face. Liston's ritual was jumping rope to the James Brown recording of "Night Train." I'd never seen someone jump rope like that. He was so big and agile, and he'd loop the rope around and swing it back and forth without missing a beat, all in time to the music. Then he worked the speed bag, hit the heavy bag, and finally laid on the ground while his trainer would drop a 16-pound medicine ball on his body.

To say that Liston had a rough background would be an understatement. His birthdate was unknown (he may have been 10 years older than he claimed), and he was the youngest of 24 kids of poor sharecroppers in Arkansas. From age eight, his father made him work the cotton fields and subjected him to severe beatings. Sonny ended up moving with his mom to St. Louis around the age 13, where he had run-ins with the law and served time in prison for armed robbery. All the fighting in prison led him to a priest who steered him into boxing as a way to remove him from criminal life, though his reputation never fully left him.

When Liston was done with his training that day, I went up and asked him for his autograph. He hesitated, and it took him more than a minute to write his name.* Then I asked him for a photograph, and we posed in a fighting stance. He was patient and quiet with me, though there was talk that he could be a mean guy. But I was in such awe at that age, I wouldn't have noticed a thing. I just couldn't believe I was standing right next to him, his fist on my chin, mine on his.

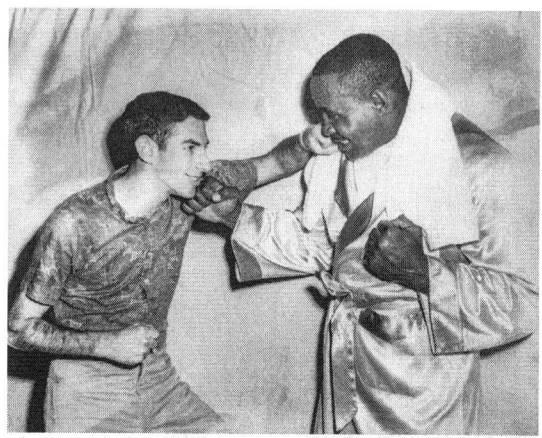

Me at 18 posing with Heavyweight Champion Sonny Liston at the Thunderbird Hotel before his rematch against Floyd Patterson.

---

* The next time I saw him, he had mimeographed autographs to hand out to fans.

I also watched Floyd Patterson train that week, but I don't remember a thing about it. Sonny Liston was so imposing even my *memory* had no room for anyone else. A little over six feet and 215 pounds with gigantic, meaty hands and a huge reach, Liston was a force—just an explosive fighter. Mike Tyson, who himself scared grown men out of their shorts, called Liston "the first intimidating fighter…a real badass menacing force."[9] Liston had once knocked out a guy's teeth in a fight that lasted less than a minute. Very few people thought Patterson had a chance.*

Sig and I, along with two of our friends, took in the Monday night fight from the $10 nosebleed seats. Since, I've sat ringside at some of the greatest fights of our time, but taking that bout in from the top row still holds a special place for me: the wide circular lights, the old-school 35MM Panasonic cameras on the media platform, the excitement like a thick presence in the air. While we waited, Sig and I were trying to point out any Hollywood stars or Rat Packers we could spot down in the front row. The fight was supposed to start at 7:30 p.m., but it was late, only drawing out the suspense. Anticipation builds in big stadiums like that, especially when you don't know what's going to happen. Before they touch gloves, everything is just a hypothetical.

The crowd of 7,500 was almost entirely on Patterson's side. Floyd was the more sympathetic figure, a polite and congenial guy and a good Catholic—which in those days mattered. Just about everyone was pulling for him; they wanted to see the underdog take down the big, bad Goliath. Liston didn't get a single cheer from the crowd, and I heard a smattering of boos. Liston was only about an inch or so taller than Patterson, but he dwarfed the former champ, almost punching down on him. He also had about 20 pounds on Floyd and took up most of the ring when he stood in the center, declaring his space. Patterson was famous for his "kangaroo punch." He'd lurch

---

* This indeed had happened, against Wayne Bethea in August, 1958

forward off the ground and swing around with this left hook that knocked opponents off their feet. But Liston never even gave him a chance to try it.

After all that build up, the fight was over in a blink. Liston knocked Patterson down three times in a little over two minutes, and it wasn't even that close. The last time he got Floyd with an uppercut and then a right that kept him down for good. When the fight ended, there was a stark silence that spread from the apron up in the stands to us. It was like a balloon had popped and took all the energy out of the arena. Patterson later said he wished there was a trap door so he could crawl out of there without having to face the crowd.*

After the knockout, Muhammad Ali, who had been in the front row in a houndstooth jacket and busy mouth, immediately climbed into the ring to taunt Liston. As Las Vegas police swarmed around Ali, he called Liston a "big ugly bear" and rhymed about how he'd take him down in eight rounds. The next year, in one of the sports' greatest moments, Ali would shock everyone by taking Liston's title after he wouldn't get off his stool for the seventh round. But that night against Patterson, Liston was still the champ, though he left the arena with his hood up to a sea of boos. The two Liston-Patterson matches lasted fewer than five minutes *combined*. That's the thing about boxing—sometimes with one punch, it's over.

It was the first heavyweight championship fight in Las Vegas, and it set a precedent. The city was a place worthy of a title fight, and casino managers saw how much money was to be made. That night, they learned that the fight crowd liked to gamble. I remember walking out to the Strip, jammed up with people looking to lose more of their money after the fight, especially since they probably felt like they didn't get their money's worth.

---

* Patterson actually used to travel with sunglasses, fake beard and mustache so he could sneak out undetected after losses.

Ringside

*The first ticket sold to the Liston versus Patterson rematch.
I showed up early to be the first in line.*

A little more than two years later, in November 1965, I saw Ali fight again—this time as heavyweight champ. He had changed his name by then and was more outwardly political, associating with the Black Muslim movement. When Ali entered the ring that night and started dancing around in his flowing white robe, a sea of boos from the 8,000 in the stands filled the space. In a few short years, he had gone from a brash but likable young boxer to a pariah. But man, I couldn't wait to see him fight.

Patterson, back after the Liston humiliations, had gone after Ali in the press, saying that no Black Muslim should be champion. Ali was angry, but likely also hurt. He had been a fan of Patterson's, even writing one of his first poems about Patterson's title reclamation from Ingemar Johansson. What ultimately pissed Ali off was that Patterson insisted on still calling him Clay, refusing to use his adopted Muslim name. Ali had been hounding Floyd all week, calling him "a rabbit," even bringing a bag of carrots to his training camp.

On fight night, Ali was jabbering nonstop at him, even during the referee's instructions. The champ was seven years younger, 16 pounds heavier, and clearly had a much further reach. Before the first bell even sounded, Ali jumped out like a man possessed, or more accurately, a

19

man wronged. He danced on the balls of his feet, getting Patterson to miss a few times and fall off balance. I remember Ali holding out his big left arm to put on Floyd's head, almost the way you'd do to a little brother who was trying to come at you. (Ali almost got disqualified for this "holding and hitting" move at the 1960 Olympics.) As the fight wore on, Ali punished Floyd in a way that was almost vengeful.[*]

From my seat in the lower balcony, I could hear Ali talking throughout the fight, "What's my name! What's my name!" he'd taunt as he moved. Ali's hands were so much faster than any boxer I'd ever seen. He was light on his feet while also packing a powerful punch. It was a deadly combination that many great fighters could not handle. Ali also stood further away but could still land punches, while Floyd was angling to get closer without getting hit. He didn't have much luck with that. Any time he got within reach, Ali made him pay.

"Like a kid pulling the wings off a butterfly," boxing writer Robert Lipsyte called the mismatch. Patterson seemed like a nice, quiet guy getting bullied. Ali carried him enough to beat him up a little bit, clowned him, toyed with him. He had actually told a reporter that his fight with Liston was unsatisfying because there's not enough for him to watch; he wanted to make sure the Patterson fight went on long enough that he could "enjoy the movie." It was stopped in the 12th round. Ali defended his title, and the champ had more than enough footage.

Ali would eventually become the most revered fighter, athlete—maybe even man—of the 20th Century, but for those of us who remember his heyday, we know that he wasn't always seen this way. At first, he was labeled a loudmouth, a young and cocky kid, and then when he dipped his toe into politics, religion, and Vietnam protest, people came out in force against him. History has proved kind to Ali, but at that time, he was a polarizing figure. He was a visionary, as a boxer and as a man. It took a while for the times to catch up to him.

---

[*] "In the fight itself, I did not have a chance," Floyd would later say, though he attributed it to a back spasm in the second round that hindered his punching.

CHAPTER THREE

■ ■ ■

The Enforcer

From an early age, sports gave me a purpose and a sense of belonging. It was a universe that I fit into and understood, which as a kid, is no small thing. I wasn't the most stylish or confident teenager, neither among my peers nor with girls. Actually, I wasn't even that great of an athlete, but being on a team gave me a sense of identity. My sister, Susan, who is a couple years younger, didn't see much of me besides at the dinner table. We lived on different planets, as many siblings do at that age, ensnared in different circles and interests. Years later, we became close, but when we first moved to Las Vegas, I was on my own. It was on the little league baseball team when I first felt a part of something and that continued with the various teams I played for during my teenage years.

My father was busy working and was not much of a sports fan, but he made an effort to show up at my games, even though I wasn't a star or even a starter. It meant a great deal to me, looking over to the sidelines and seeing him (and my mother) sitting in those metal bleachers. Years later, I made sure to do the same for my children, mostly for my son who played basketball into college. It mattered to me that he, too, could look over from the court and see me. I wanted to be that kind of father.

My mother was a loving and gentle woman, a Jewish housewife with a slight Virginia lilt in her voice. She expected us all to be home to have family dinner at 6 p.m., played mahjong with friends in the neighborhood, and helped out at our temple as a member of the "Sisterhood." By the time I went to college at University of Nevada Southern (now UNLV), I reveled in the freedom—no one was expecting me home for family dinner—but I found that I missed what my mother created. She had built a stable home, a world in which I felt safe. I was surprised to find that freedom wasn't the be-all, end-all.

After my freshman year, I transferred to University of Nevada Reno, a few hundred miles north of Las Vegas. It was a declaration of my independence, leaving my hometown like that, giving me some breathing room from my family. Southern Nevada felt like an extension of high school—the same people doing the same things. My friend Sig and I decided to branch out. We became roommates in Reno and pledged the Sigma Alpha Epsilon (SAE) fraternity. I enjoyed the camaraderie, even going through hazing, which was pretty brutal at the time.

Sig was a popular and charismatic guy, handsome and confident with girls. It wasn't long before he became the fraternity's president. Politics was in his blood. Years later he became an influential Republican strategist, media advisor, and ultimately U.S. ambassador in the George H.W. Bush White House. We were a tandem at Reno. When Sig became editor of the school newspaper, "The Sagebrush," I became business manager. I was the treasurer of SAE, and he was the president. Years later, we spent time working in advertising together before I made boxing my career.

I played baseball at Nevada Southern (I mostly shagged foul balls for the starters) and was a long jumper for University of Nevada-Reno. It was the mid-1960s, and though I was not the traditional hippie, I was a rock-'n'-roll fan who sported longer hair, a t-shirt, and blue jeans—the uniform of counterculture. On a trip out to Haight-Ashbury in San Francisco, I got a front row look at the hippie movement. I might've liked their style and music, but I was always more mainstream. A rule follower, I guess. It's no coincidence I'd eventually set and enforce rules for a living. Asthma kept me out of Vietnam, and being a general straight arrow kept me away from drugs and rebellion.

After graduating Nevada Reno in 1966 with a business degree, the plan was obvious: take a job at my father's beauty supply company. To learn the manufacturing end of the business, first I took a job with Helene Curtis, a cosmetics company in Chicago. I hit the road, traveling up and down Illinois to beauty shops and salons with salesmen. It was a grooming period, so to speak. After a year, I came home to Las Vegas to join the family business. Part of the job was keeping up with the soap operas on TV so I could engage in casual chitchat with the hairdressers. I was 23 years old, and my life seemed fairly carved out and predetermined. It was nothing too exciting, but it was steady and dependable.

But I got set on an alternate route, one I never could have conceived of. That fall, after I returned from a year in the Midwest, I noticed an advertisement in the "Las Vegas Sun" newspaper.

Football Fans!
Do you watch games and yell at the referees? Do you think you could do better?
Come down to an orientation meeting this Sunday at Las Vegas High School and see if you have what it takes to be an official.*

I had long been drawn to the spirit of competition, the glory of the man in the arena, the camaraderie of teams, and the courageous drive for glory. After I came back to Las Vegas, I played city league basketball and slow pitch softball, which were really the only options

---

* The actual advertisement is lost to memory, but this was the gist of it.

for someone my age. Being an official was an opportunity to be part of the game—not as spectator, but an integral facet of it all. The official is the grounding force of any sport. Without him, it's just a bunch of guys running around. That Sunday, I went to the orientation, as a lark really, never thinking about what it would one day lead to.

I found out pretty quickly that I didn't know as much as I thought. I assumed I had all the rules of football down, and later basketball and baseball, but I couldn't have been more wrong. Everyone thinks they know the rules until they actually sit down and read a rule book. Besides all the details of a sport I'd followed my whole life, I learned important elements like mechanics: getting out of the way (you can get roughed up pretty easily if you're in the wrong place) and being in position to see the play. Officials' movements are structured and choreographed; they're not just running up and down the field aimlessly. Not unlike an offensive lineman or shortstop, I had to learn where to be in all situations.

The other key element for the official is communication—the way you interact with the coaches and the players. A good official must be able to explain himself, to talk to coaches when they're mad (*especially* when they're mad) and know how to *not* escalate a situation. It's about imparting a sense of calm and knowing that if the player or coach needs to vent, you need to let them. Of course, there is a line. A good rule of thumb is if they start to make it personal (claiming that *you*—rather than the call you made—are "f***ing terrible"), then you throw a flag or toss them. Officials who are thin-skinned and react immediately are not long for that world. But I was a good fit. I had a natural affinity for sports, the right demeanor, and didn't care if I wasn't the center of attention. Later, when I became a boxing regulator, I already had experience not taking the spotlight. I didn't want it. The spotlight is for the athletes.

After a few years refereeing Pop Warner youth football, I started officiating junior high basketball and softball. Then I moved up the ranks to high school football games and then state championships. Once, as a line judge at a high school football game, the receiver was running to the end zone, and I backpedaled down the sideline to keep up with him. It was just an instinct, but I got reamed by the coach for showing up his player. I had violated the cardinal rule: if you notice the official, he has done something wrong.

Through the 1970s, I worked for my father's beauty supply business. It was a great joy to work every day with my father, who passed away in 1979. We named my first son Heiden after him (and he went on to name his son Heiden, as well). He didn't get to see what became of my sports officiating and boxing career.

I was visiting something like 80 beauty shops a week. I'd ask what they needed, take orders for supplies, and talk to different hairdressers. I was more of an order taker than salesman, the young guy selling hairpins or permanent weaves. At the Caesars Palace salon, there was a girl at the front desk named Jody. She moved on from the front desk to become a hairdresser/manicurist and then a manager. She was demure, sophisticated with her hair pulled back to show her beautiful face. For months, I tried to talk with her, though I was very shy. She was popular among men, and I'd make jokes like, "Tell me when the decks are clear so I can call you." I was intimidated by her beauty, but soon I asked her out. We start going on dates—movies and dinner. I remember giving her a ring to be engaged, maybe to buy myself time. But we married soon after.

I was lucky that Jody understood that sports were part of my life, and officiating had a claim on my time. On weekends and nights, I was out on the field or on the court with my whistle, wearing my black and whites, calling football games or sitting at the scorer's table at UNLV basketball games running the shot clock (which I still do to this day). By the 1980s, I had moved on to junior college games in Southern Utah and drove to Southern California for Division III football, but I still loved working high school football. I became a Division I football official in 1987 and worked for 19 years in the PCAA, Big West, WAC and Mountain West Conferences. I was selected to work three bowl games: The Independence Bowl in Shreveport, Louisiana, The Aloha Hawaii Bowl in Honolulu and the Cotton Bowl in Dallas. Officiating was never my primary career. A high school paid around $40 a game, and college games paid $600 for a few hours of work. But by the early 1980s, officiating was just as much a part of me as anything else.

■ ■ ■

During that time, my love for boxing never waned. I'd always carried this romantic view of a sport that is inherently violent. Living in Las Vegas was a dreamland for a fight fan. I caught all the big heavyweights of that era: Foreman, Norton, Holmes, and of course, Ali. I was there, with better seats this time, when a 36-year-old Ali was upset by 1976 Olympic gold medalist Leon Spinks to win the heavyweight title. Six months later, they had a rematch, and Ali regained the heavyweight title for the third time. Ali was slower then—not the brash creature of years past—but he was still a sight to see. Nobody moved or hit like Ali. He was in a class by himself.

Boxing offers a rare thing: one-on-one combat, no teammates to hide behind, two people with no barrier and nothing but their fists. There's also a historical, almost elemental, nature of fights, coming from a tradition which stretches back to dueling and codes of honor from medieval times. The term "ring" actually comes from the fact that early fights took place inside a ring drawn in the dirt, and a ring of people would watch the contest.

So, my life was boxing and football on the weekends and beauty supplies during the week—as polar opposite as you could get, now that I think back on it. As a referee, boxing officials and judges were in my orbit, part of a tight-knit community. I refereed football games with a few of them, and my old friend Sig was a boxing commissioner for the state of Nevada by the time I started working for his advertising firm in the early 1980s. I could afford better seats for the big fights at the Convention Center by then, but I still took in the smaller fights at the Silver Slipper. Whenever I'd run into guys I knew in the boxing game, we'd get talking. That's likely when the thought of actually working in boxing first trickled into my mind.

Another close friend of mine, Chuck Minker, was a world-class boxing judge who worked 27 title fights including Ali-Holmes and Leonard-Hearns. We coached and played softball together and both worked UNLV basketball games—him on the game clock and me on the shot clock. "Marc," he said to me one time, "you love going to the fights. Why not become an inspector and work in the back rooms?"

I'd been to enough boxing matches in my life to have an interest, knowledge and passion. My teenage self would have jumped at the idea of working in gyms and dressing rooms, going to fights for free and being part of this world I loved. So, I put an application in with the athletic commission. I didn't hear a thing. They had too many, or they didn't accept it that first year.

But, the second year, in 1985, I was in. I started my tenure in the boxing world.

I began in the trenches as a per-diem inspector, whose main job is to watch the fighters before the fight to make sure nothing fishy is going on. What to look for is second nature to me now, but I learned everything I know about wraps, gloves, cuts, and cornermen inside Johnny Tocco's Ringside Gym. Tocco was a Las Vegas institution unto himself, a cigar-smoking guy from St. Louis with grey hair, heavy-lidded blue eyes, and a prominent nose. The story was he had come west to Las Vegas in the 1950s to watch a fight and never left. Back in the day he had been Sonny Liston's trainer (he grew up in St. Louis), and he knew everyone and everything by the time I walked into his gym.

Tocco's Ringside Gym was an important part of boxing lore. Though it was literally only about 10 minutes away, it was as far from places like MGM Grand and Caesars Palace as you could get. Inside the gyms like Johnny's is an aspect of both Las Vegas and of boxing that few people get to see. But it's an integral part of the sport, and it's where many fighters get their starts. Places like that lay the groundwork for all the pomp and circumstance of fighting under the bright lights. Training at Johnny Tocco's was a rite of passage. The smart ones—guys like Bernard Hopkins—kept going back to places like that even after they had made it, just to stoke the fire. It's a place where champs and nobodies train next to each other, and no one cares who you are or how many knockouts you have.

Tocco's Ringside Gym was a brutally hot place, which is how Johnny liked it. He believed that fighters should sweat, *needed* to sweat—so there was no air conditioning, not even an open window. (I believed the windows were nailed shut, just to make sure no one got any ideas.) There were metal bars on the doors, old fight posters and mirrors on the walls, cigar smoke lingering in the air, and not a tourist to be found. I loved it in there: the smell of liniment mixed with sweat, the thudding of the heavy bag, the leather-on-leather smack of sparring, the flick-flick sound of the speed bag, the old trainers yelling at their fighters. It was tight and cramped, and Johnny's office in the back was a cluttered mess where you couldn't even tell if you were standing on the floor.

When I was first hired as an inspector with the Nevada State Athletic Commission in 1985, I met with Johnny, like everyone did. He showed me the ropes (no pun intended) and it all started with the hands. In boxing, a fight between two people is really between their four hands. So, the inspector has to watch the fighter's hands being wrapped to make sure there's nothing hidden inside his gloves. Johnny walked us through the proper way to wrap (up to six feet of tape and 15 yards of gauze per hand), how gloves were to be put on, and what to watch out for in the corners during a fight. He knew every trick, scam and shortcut. He demonstrated how cornermen could wrap illegally, either by putting on too much tape or by taping over the knuckles. He knew what they could hide in gauze and how some even wet the tape so it became like a plaster cast, which would feel like a concrete punch. Hand wrapping is literally an ancient art, going back 8,000 years to the Egyptians and Greeks who did it before fights. Fighters' hands are their livelihood, and they entrust their cornermen to be protectors of their invaluable assets.

Johnny also taught us which cut solutions were illegal, how much Vaseline was allowed on the face, and how to spot signs during a fight that a trainer could be sneaking something into a water bottle or sneaking in smelling salts (signs like a fighter's head snapping back). Another part of my job was administering drug tests. I had to follow fighters into the bathroom and collect their urine specimen after the fight. I actually had to watch them urinate to make sure they weren't cheating, switching out the specimen or doing any other tricks. It's a sad truth: there will always be those looking for an advantage.

Johnny was a no-nonsense guy who had seen just about everything, and every conversation with him was an education. Guys like him embodied the history, knowledge and tradition of boxing. Trainers like Johnny are the ones that kept boxing alive from era to era. They're living history books.

CHAPTER FOUR

■ ■ ■

Eyes on the Corner

"The best thing that ever happens to an athlete is being invited to Las Vegas to box."

—George Foreman[10]

On the night of April 6, 1987, I got a chance to play a role in boxing history as an inspector for Sugar Ray Leonard versus Marvin Hagler. Of course, I was a footnote—an aspect of the scenery as far as the crowd was concerned. But, being part of it was still one of the most thrilling moments of my professional life.

Like many, I had known of Leonard before he went pro. He was a star of the 1976 Olympics in Montreal, which I saw firsthand. I watched that stellar USA boxing team, which included both Michael and Leon Spinks, and was on hand when Ray won gold. He was so quick, and his hand speed was so fast that everyone knew he would soon be fighting for the title. Though he promised not to go pro, insisting he wanted to do something else with his life, the call was too loud and the pull too magnetic. Three years after his gold medal performance, I watched him defeat Wilfred Benitez for the welterweight title at Caesars Palace in the tennis pavilion. I believe I was one of the few who saw him win both the gold medal and the world championship in person.

It certainly didn't hurt Ray's career that he was also a confident and good-looking guy with a sense of how to sell himself. He was one of those rare crossover stars who appealed to women and non-fight fans. Unfortunately, Leonard's career was cut short a few years after winning the belt. He was forced to retire due to a detached retina in his left eye. The Hagler fight that April night was to be his big return. He made a lot of comments in the press about how he was only coming out of retirement to fight Hagler, how that was all he wanted to do.

The backstory had all the drama you'd want out of a big fight. Hagler, the champ at the time, had been in Leonard's shadow for many years as they were first coming up. Promoters were throwing money at Leonard to fight back then, while Hagler, a Brockton native, was shut out for so long that he enlisted big-name Massachusetts politicians Tip O'Neill and Ted Kennedy to help him get a title shot. Promoter Bob Arum and others were served notice that they had to give Hagler a title shot, or else there'd be an investigation. Hagler got his chance and became champion soon thereafter. Hagler no doubt saw the Leonard fight as a way to prove himself to all those who had ignored him while instead rolling out the red carpet for the handsome Olympic champion. It may have been in the past, but as far as Hagler was concerned, it may as well have been yesterday. Boxers have long memories. All the great athletes do.

The contrast of their personalities—the flashy, preening Leonard versus the blue collar, snarling Hagler—made for dramatic tension. Leonard was a man who punched people for a living and carried himself like a movie star. Hagler was a millionaire who carried himself like a working-class guy. The smart money was on Hagler, who had knocked out 11 straight opponents, while Leonard was rusty from three years off, with only one fight in the past five years. Plus, he was fighting in a heavier weight class (middleweight), after a career as a welterweight. No one thought Leonard had a chance at beating Hagler—but everyone wanted to see him try.

The big event was preceded by a multi-city promotional tour by the fighters and their camps. The closed-circuit broadcast of the fight was shown in 600 theaters worldwide—all of them sold out. It was also the first big Pay-Per-View fight, launching that lucrative era when big title matches were brought into people's homes. Hagler-Leonard was an event, a showdown between two world-class boxers, a match that harkened back to the iconic title fights I grew up on. It was both the past and the future. Bob Arum, Hagler's irrepressible promoter, dubbed it "The Superfight."

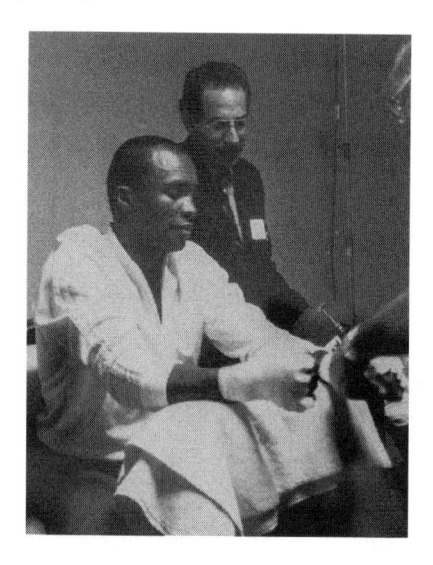

Observing Sugar Ray Leonard getting his hands wrapped before the legendary 1987 "Superfight" versus Marvin Hagler.

The fight was outdoors at Caesars Palace, which is the most magical venue in all of sports. I've been to the Super Bowl, the World Series, and to just about all the other big sports events. A title fight outdoors at Caesars Palace blows them all away. Ask anyone else in the boxing world, and they'll tell you the same. Other Las Vegas hotels like the Hilton and the Dunes had outdoor fights, but none had the dramatic ambience of a fight Caesars Palace.

By the time of the main event, when the sky darkened and the stars glittered above, you could feel it in your bones. The atmosphere was both grandiose and intimate, with anticipation bubbling in the veins of 15,000 people. The big flag was unfurled and flapped over the hotel, and the rig of lights was squared above the ring, shining on the two fighters. In a stadium setting, you usually lose that intimacy, but Caesars Palace always maintained it. In reality, it was in a parking lot with a wooden arena, temporary bleachers, and floor seats, but the whole added up to so much more. If I close my eyes, I can put myself back there.

In the evening, I picked up Leonard's gloves at ringside and walked over to his dressing room to deliver them. I was nervous, of course. The dressing rooms for Leonard-Hagler were in the tennis pavilion past the hotel, a small metal shed with two rooms, separated by thin drywall. I knocked as I stepped into the tight space and spotted Ray and his trainer, the incomparable Angelo Dundee. Angelo was as much of a legend in the boxing world as any fighter. He had been Ali's trainer, a Damon-Runyon-type figure of the old boxing world, like a character out of a storybook. He had the stories of the legends, some of whom he helped to make. Angelo had a good sense of humor and knew to be loose, keeping it light in the dressing room. As he wrapped Ray's hands, he wasn't talking strategy. Strategy had been set in the weeks and months before. Dundee was focused on building Ray's confidence, pattering alongside Mike Trainer, Ray's agent and longtime right-hand man.

I was new enough to the job that I couldn't believe I was in that small room with these guys, along with Ray's son, Ray Jr., a telegenic kid I recognized from a 7UP commercial. To be in there with legends, getting to hand Ray his gloves, was surreal. It was like stepping into one of my dreams, being that close to it, being *part* of it. I had to force myself to remember I was working. After the wrapping, Angelo got up and started getting Ray pumped. He walked over to the thin walls and started banging on them, yelling, "You're an old man, Marvin! We're gonna kick your ass!"

An hour later, I took my seat in front, a long way from the

nosebleeds where Sig and I took in Liston-Patterson 25 years earlier. The energy in the crowd was intense, a recognition that we were about to witness two all-timers go at it for the first time. After Leonard came into the ring with his crew, Hagler entered to what had become his theme song, Edwin Starr's "War."

War.
What is it good for?
Absolutely nothing!

My seat was a stool in the corner next to Leonard's team, which was not a perk but a necessity. (People who knew me asked me afterward, "What were *you* doing up there? You're not a doctor.") As an inspector, after each round, I had to climb up on the apron and watch Leonard's corner. I would quickly shoot up the stairs and get a good spot on the ropes as Angelo talked to Ray.

"I want you smooth, baby!" Angelo yelled at Leonard after the first round. "Smooth, you get me!"

Angelo kept Ray focused and confident, reminding him to get in flurries at the end of the rounds to influence the judges, while also staying away from Hagler's power. Hagler was a lefty but he could surprise opponents by deftly switching back and forth, which confused the hell out of fighters, In fact, Hagler began that fight as a righty ("orthodox") only to switch later on, though some thought it was too late.

Being in the corner flavored the way I watched the fight, but I thought Leonard was brilliant that night. He managed to stay away for most of the 12 rounds, and Hagler just got increasingly frustrated. Leonard would always move, making it harder for Hagler's punches to land, a strategy that ultimately tired out the champ. The first four rounds clearly belonged to Leonard, but then Hagler came out like a beast in the fifth round. After that, it see-sawed back and forth to the end, but it sure seemed as though Leonard got more punches in. As

Angelo instructed, Ray would fight the last 30 to 45 seconds to steal the round and get the judges' attention.

When the final bell rang at the end Round 12, both fighters put their hands up in victory. Hagler uncharacteristically began dancing around the ring. Ray answered by standing up on the ropes of his corner to pose for the crowd. They both thought they had won, and it was almost like they were lobbying, though the scores were already in. After the drama and action, we all stewed in that heavy suspense. No one knew who won until Chuck Hull said the words "new" before champion. At that point, Leonard's corner erupted, as did the crowd.

Hagler's split decision loss remains controversial to this day. Many felt he was robbed, no one more so than Hagler, who never fought again—never even put on gloves again. He retired and moved to Italy, 30 years later still insisting he won that fight. JoJo Guerra, the judge who overwhelmingly ruled in favor of Leonard—handing him the belt—never got to judge another big U.S. fight. Bob Arum made sure of that.

I was incredibly lucky to begin my boxing career during that famed era. Besides Leonard-Hagler, there was also Tommy "The Hit Man" Hearns and Roberto Duran who encompassed what many called "the last golden age" of boxing.[11] They weren't heavyweights, but they were superstars who helped keep the sport in the public consciousness. Those four had nine memorable fights that decade, and some said that they saved boxing in the post-Ali era.[12] I always have a nostalgic view of that night, my first big fight, and I loved playing a small part in it.

In 1987, my friend Chuck Minker retired as a boxing judge to become Executive Director of the Nevada State Athletic Commission. Soon after, he made me Chief Inspector. The inspector job was just about every weekend, 50 fights a year, with the occasional weekday fight card. For big fights, promoters liked to have other fights around the big event, so we'd sometimes have fights Thursday, Friday, and Saturday night, which could get cumbersome. But it was the fulfillment of a childhood dream and a labor of love. My family understood.

The chief inspector job paid a $1,000 a month, a lot of money back then for a part-time gig. I was in charge of all the other inspectors, responsible for assigning their fights, paying the fighters, and delivering gloves. Delivering gloves was not just ceremonial. A few years earlier in New York, boxer Luis Resto's trainer, Panama Lewis, had removed the cushion from his gloves, damaging up-and-comer Billy Collins so much that it ended his career.

Chuck mentored me, and through him, I learned how the commission was run: the ins and outs of scheduling fights, choosing judges and referees, dealing with promoters, and licensing fighters. All the wheels that had to keep spinning for the sport to work. I did my best to be his eyes and ears and to make him look good. Meanwhile, he was grooming me for a job I would one day have. Neither of us thought it would come so soon.

Later that year, I was on hand when Tommy Hearns fought Sugar Ray Leonard at Caesars Palace for a rematch of the epic fight they'd had eight years earlier, a loss Hearns wanted to avenge. Hearns was openly calling the rematch "payback," and it was a long time in the making. Both fighters were slower by that point, but still quicker and stronger than most boxers in their prime. Hearns was especially impressive and always a threat to knock a guy out. In "Fight Town," Tim Dahlberg writes about the time that Hearns knocked out Clyde Gray while Hearns was moving *backward*, an almost impossible task. It's a testament to how much raw punching power he had.

About an hour before the scheduled fight, Chuck gave me the gloves to take down to the dressing rooms. Fighters like to warm up with their gloves on, so I always made a point of getting there early. I never wanted any fighter to say he didn't have enough time to properly warm up.

In Hearns' dressing room, the atmosphere was hyped. Hearns' camp was raucous, yelling and barking, doing a call-and-response routine. His trainer would say, "What time is it!?" and others would respond, "It's Hearns Time!" They were feeding off each other's energy, collectively amplifying one another. Ray's team was more subdued, especially since he had cut ties with Angelo Dundee, who was always good for a couple of noisy admonishments.

Billed "The War" by Bob Arum, the fight would unify the super middleweight belts.* The crowd was full of celebrities that June night, including Michael Jordan and Charles Barkley, among other luminaries from sports, entertainment, and business. It was a close fight, a back-and-forth, but Hearns clearly overpowered him, knocking Leonard down twice. By the end, Hearns got tired legs, and Leonard took advantage, making a final last push that certainly saved him from a loss. The fight ended in a controversial draw, and the crowd—solidly in Hearns' camp—lost their collective mind.

"Bullshit! Bullshit!" the crowd bellowed within minutes of the decision. In "Four Kings," George Kimball writes about how all the bettors tossed away their slips that night, assuming they had lost. The custodial crew were able to cash in the tickets and make off with quite a haul. Years later, Leonard admitted that Hearns—who knocked him down twice—should've won the fight. Hearns, who fought for another 17 years, no doubt agreed.

---

* Arum also hired both Duran and Hagler to do commentary, so all four greats were present that night.

CHAPTER FIVE

■ ■ ■

Hands on the Canvas

"If a boxing match is a story, it is an always wayward story, one in which anything can happen...In no other sports can so much take place in so brief a period of time, and so irrevocably."

—Joyce Carol Oates[13]

In 1991 my close friend Chuck Minker, Executive Director of the Nevada State Athletic Commission (NSAC), became ill. (NSAC ran boxing in the state, and because of Las Vegas' role in the sport, Chuck held a hugely influential position).

Though he didn't smoke, Chuck was diagnosed with a rare form of lung cancer, so I began to fill in for him on an interim basis. The next year, at the young age of 42, Chuck passed away—a blow to all of us who knew and loved him. At his funeral, I gave one of his eulogies, talking about my friendship with a man who was all class, whom no one could say a bad word about. Many people came out to celebrate Chuck's life—from the heights of the boxing world to the back office at the commission to friends and family. A big sports complex in Las Vegas was named in Chuck's memory, a gesture that recognized how central he was to the sports community in Las Vegas and to the boxing world at large.

Minker was an exceptional teacher as well, and at his side, I learned the world of boxing regulation, the finer points of the sport, and the way an executive director should act. For one thing, at the fighters' weigh-in, which Chuck always conducted, he made sure to stay invisible. "Don't ever get in front of the scale," he would remind me. "Make sure your back is always to the cameras." This was fundamental: the spotlight should always be on the fighters. When he became ill, I filled in for him conducting the weigh-ins. I told him, "I'll always face the scale, in your honor." Sometimes the weighers stand right in front between the fighters; you see their faces and they're part of the show. So, I would do my business and then duck down to get off camera. To this day when I conduct weigh-ins, if it's a regular meat scale, I keep my back to my camera—in honor of Chuck.

In 1993, the five-member Nevada commission, along with the governor, appointed me as Executive Director. I was honored to take over for my friend and mentor. Boxing went from an avocation to a vocation, so I had to quit my advertising job. Now I was in boxing full time, which was an adjustment, though a background in public relations and advertising helped with some aspects of the job. There was a lot of learning early on: state procedures, budgeting, scheduling, and technicalities. I was fortunate to have a staff who made sure I never dropped the ball.

A fight was usually prepared eight weeks in advance, during which the commission gets approvals and medicals, which all culminates in fight week. When I first got to the commission, I would've been lost without Sandy Johnson and Colleen Patchin, who guided me through what is a busy and complex office. Later, Daisy Negron and Barbara Barrios also became indispensable to me. The commission ran on their hard work: checking medicals, keeping schedules, dealing with the state budget, working with the commissioners, and helping to run and record the meetings. Everyone had a job to do, and I showed up every day knowing they would help me do mine. I loved working with them, and I couldn't have worked without them. They weren't all boxing fans when I got there, but by the time I left, they sure were. The two chief inspectors under me were Chuck Sledge and Tony Lato, both total pros who assisted me at the weigh-ins, scheduled the inspectors, and made sure fight night ran smoothly.

During my time as Executive Director, I worked for two outstanding commission chairmen, who alternated throughout the years. Dr. James Nave is a native Missourian, with a distinct Southern accent and approachable demeanor. Intelligent, direct, and trustworthy, Dr. Nave has long been a mentor and friend to me. He is also a preeminent veterinarian, and this is how I first knew him. Before his time with the commission, he was a doctor who happened to be a longtime boxing fan. Back when I was working as chief inspector, I'd take the family dog to his office for a check-up and chat with him about past or upcoming fight. Because I used to bring the upcoming fight's gloves home with me—so no one could tamper with them—they were always in my trunk the day before the fight. Once, before a big Tommy Hearns fight at Caesars Palace, I took them out to show Nave. Though Dr. Nave hadn't told anyone yet, the governor was about to appoint him to the commission. It was pretty foolish of me to show anyone the gloves like that, and we laughed about it afterward. Throughout our time working together, Nave was always supportive, willing to take the heat for any decision I made. We'd go watch fights together, and he remains a friend to this day.

The other chairman during my time at the commission was the famous and beloved Dr. Elias Ghanem. Dr. Ghanem was an elegant and worldly doctor to the stars—from Elvis to Michael Jackson—and a close acquaintance of influential people like former President Bill Clinton. He was handsome and debonair with a cosmopolitan air about him. Whenever I brought an issue to him, he'd say in his Lebanese accent, "No problem, baby."

While Dr. Nave possessed the more subtle, hang-in-the background style, Dr. Ghanem relished being the face of the commission. But he was also a trailblazer in many ways, instrumental in getting the Nevada commission to the forefront of HIV testing for fighters. Every licensed Nevada fighter went to his office, and he did thousands of HIV (and Hepatitis B and C) tests—at no charge. Well-regarded fight doctor Dr. Flip Homansky played an integral role in this, as well. By ensuring the sport was medically safe, by committing to things that other sports weren't doing at the time, Dr. Ghanem helped strengthen boxing. He had the ease and skills of a diplomat and was the man who could always get both sides together, which is not always easy to do in boxing.

In 2001, Dr. Ghanem fell ill from the cancer he'd been battling for a few years, but he continued to work as chairman. I would go over to his house and let him know what was going on with the upcoming fights and he would regale me with stories of his various youthful adventures. He passed away that August and left a giant mark on the boxing world, the medical field and Las Vegas as a whole. I can still hear him to this day, coolly responding to some thorny issue I had brought to him. "No problem, baby."

My job entailed making recommendations for officials, maintaining a presence at public events, meting out punishment when needed (and answering for that decision), and acting as a liaison between the boxing community and the commission. Of course, in boxing, you also have to deal with promoters, who are the engine of the sport on the professional level. Promoters play a huge role in that they have to sell fights and their fighters: to the commission, to the boxing world, and to the public. For many decades, there were two names who stood atop the promotion game, both larger than life: Bob Arum and Don King.

King and Arum weren't necessarily enemies, but they certainly butted heads from time to time, going after each other in the press and in court, trying to steal each other's fighters. The men were a study in contrasts. Arum was a hardened, experienced professional; King was the hot-tempered showman. "Think of King as a sledgehammer, and Arum as a stiletto,"[14] the great fight doctor Ferdie Pacheco once said.

The night of the Leonard-Hagler fight in 1987, my first big one as inspector, Arum and King got into a tussle ringside. After Leonard's victory, King—who was there as a spectator—tried to climb into the ring and celebrate with the new champ. An agitated Arum didn't want King inching in on his fight, so he grabbed King's tuxedo, tearing the coat. King, who almost doubled Arum in size, was escorted out by Caesars Palace security before he could respond.

The ruddy-cheeked Arum, who was part of boxing lore, had a strong accent and stronger opinions. Born into an orthodox Jewish family in Brooklyn, he began as a Harvard-educated lawyer who knew nothing about boxing. While working in the tax division for the U.S. Department of Justice Department in 1962, Arum was asked by Bobby Kennedy to seize the $5 million in funds—a king's ransom at the time—from the first Liston-Patterson fight, which shady lawyer Roy Cohn was planning to hide in Europe. The experience gave Arum a taste of the boxing world, and he liked it.

Because of the guy Arum was, he only wanted to get into the fight game if it was alongside "the only name who mattered," Muhammad Ali. A few years later, NFL legend Jim Brown introduced Arum to the champ. After getting the approval of the fighter's Black Muslim confidantes, Arum was hired as Ali's promoter. His first fight was Ali versus George Chuvalo in March 1966. The match was originally scheduled for Chicago against a different fighter, but ended up in Toronto after Ali made his first public remarks against the Vietnam War and had trouble finding a city that would take the fight. Arum promoted the match on his Diners Club credit card, after which he ended up in about $30,000 in debt.[15] But his bet paid off big.

Arum went on to work for Ali's Main Bout company, getting credit for many of Ali's stunts, though he admitted they all came from the boxer himself. The role put Arum at the center of the boxing world, a place he never really relinquished. In the 1970s,

Arum co-founded Top Rank Boxing, which remains at the top of the fight world. After Ali's retirement in the early 1980s, Arum was a part of just about all the big welterweight and middleweight fights of that era—the ones that made stars out of Hagler, Hearns, Duran, and Leonard.

Don King's path to boxing was not just different from Arum's, it was different from just about anyone's. He grew up in Cleveland, and for many years, worked as an enforcer for an illicit gambling racket, a job that landed him in prison after he beat a guy to death. Almost four years behind bars changed him. After studying in there (everything from Shakespeare to P.T. Barnum), he emerged an eloquent and gregarious showman, "having mastered a new language of his own creation, a dazzling locution that combined Ebonics with polysyllabic malapropisms,"[16] according to writer George Kimball.

A year after his release, King promoted an Ali exhibition fight at a Cleveland hospital, which he used to launch his own career. King also went on to work as Ali's promoter and made his name on some of the biggest fights of the 1970s: the 1974 Ali-Foreman fight in Zaire headlined as "The Rumble in the Jungle," Ali's match with Chuck Wepner that went the distance (the inspiration for "Rocky"), and the Ali-Frazier bout billed as the "Thrilla in Manila.". King's colorful attire, wild shock of white hair, cigars and catch phrases ("Only in America!") became part of his persona.

Mr. A and Mr. DK, as I always called them, had to work together, but it was no secret that they didn't always get along. They joined forces for a brief moment in the early 1980s for a company called BADK, but it broke up after one joint fight (Duran-Leonard I). Arum called King a "snake in the grass, that low and scurrilous cad."[17] Though they were known as rivals, they actually didn't promote that many fights together. One was the 1999 bout between Felix Trinidad and Oscar De La Hoya, in which Felix had Don and Oscar had Arum. That time, it was mutually beneficial for them to get along and co-promote the fight, billed in classic understatement as the "Fight of the Millennium." It made more money than any fight in history at the time, and in the press, it was almost like a battle of the two promoters. Most people, including Arum, thought Oscar won that fight, but Trinidad got the decision. At the post-fight press conference, King relished in claiming, "The lights are going out in Arum-ville," which aggravated Arum to no end.

If Mr. A or Mr. DK wanted to meet for lunch—to discuss an upcoming fight or anything else—I'd always pay for my own meal and often theirs. I was the face of the commission, so I couldn't even have the appearance of impropriety. King often went to talk directly to the commissioners, but when we did meet, I did a lot of listening, as Mr. DK was never short on things to say. Arum and I would talk politics, about his time in the Justice Department, and about and New York football. While King had more of the performer in him, Arum spoke more like a lawyer, which he is.

I remember the Thursday press conference for the De La Hoya-Shane Mosley fight in which Arum lauded and introduced me as the representative of "the best commission in the world." After Oscar lost a close decision that weekend, Arum spouted off to the "Las Vegas Sun" against the commission, the judges, and the integrity of the fight, so I invited him to lunch so we could talk it out. The two of us sat across from each other over a couple of juicy steaks at Ruth's Chris, and I explained how we went about the judges' selection and my feelings about the job they had done. He let me know his feelings about the third judge, the one who tipped the fight toward Mosley. Mr. A might have used some colorful language to express his discontent. At a press conference the next week, I made a crack. "Last week, we were the best commission in the world. This week we're the worst." Arum had that effect on people. I took it in stride—not everyone was going to be happy with every outcome. I remember once joking that I was going to change my name to "The Beleaguered Marc Ratner." Arum did eventually publicly apologize, which was the right thing to do. He avoided a disciplinary hearing, though there were controversies.

During the week of the Trinidad-De La Hoya fight, Chairman Nave met with just King (representing Trinidad) at Dr. Nave's house. When Arum found out, he was enraged, calling it "an ex parte meeting." I had to talk him down. Arum wasn't a grudge-holding guy—you couldn't be in our business—so by the next time I saw him, he was over it. I'm sure it had more to do with King than with anything the commission had done, but we often got caught in between the two of them.

When I think of Arum, I also remember one night at Bally's early in my tenure when I was paying fighters after a night of matches. It was a mostly Hispanic undercard, and in the process of paying everyone, I mistakenly mixed up a fighter's check. Arum tracked me down and went off. "You paid the wrong f***ing Mexican!" he screamed at me. By that time everyone had left, so we had to reimburse Top Rank, and Chairman Nave gave me a check to give to Mr. A the next day. It was an embarrassing moment for me, and Mr. A let me have it.

Don King didn't have different versions of himself. As far as I could tell, he was exactly the same across the a table as he was in front of a camera—colorful language, loud boasts, and acrobatic wordplay. Having had many conversations with Mr. DK, I can attest there was no off switch—the persona and person melded into one. He was a theatrical guy, the exact opposite of Arum, and I liked being around him. Despite some controversies, I thought he was good for the sport. He helped shine a light on the fighters, which was really the definition of his job.

Though their outrageous personalities always got the headlines, Arum and King were on top because they had the best fighters. (To this day, Arum, now 88 years old, has a huge stable, including Tyson Fury). They also knew how to talk and use the press. All boxing writers were enamored with them because they were a treasury of great stories. As much as punching and footwork, that's what boxing is about—the stories.

■ ■ ■

On the other end of the spectrum from the bright lights and press conferences were the young fighters sweating in dusky gyms, looking for their chance to go pro. These guys didn't get attention, but they were "the blood and bones of the sport,"[18] in the words of boxing writer Katherine Dunn. As the gatekeeper for boxers in the state of Nevada who desired to go pro, I spent a lot of time in those off-the-Strip places getting a good look at the next generation of fighters.

The spectacle and high drama were at the title fights, but I also loved the smaller "club" fights. In my 21 years in boxing, I went to more than I can count—not just in Las Vegas but all over the state in Laughlin, Reno, and Lake Tahoe. In Las Vegas, The Orleans Hotel & Casino was a great spot to catch club fights, which were held in the ballroom, with fold-out chairs on the four sides of the ring. The Orleans had crowds of around 2,000 and reminded me of places like the Silver Slipper from the 1960s. Championship fights are very expensive, but at the smaller places, fight fans could see good action up close for $25.

Club fights were televised, and the fighters were professional, but there was less spectacle and noise. They are a great avenue to get experience, as an inspector, judge, referee, or fighter. Some of these smaller matches are to build a prospect's record, some are for fighters at the end of their careers trying to hang on, and some are for unknowns who are trying to be discovered. Almost all fighters start out in smaller shows to get experience. Even future champion Floyd Mayweather Jr. made his pro debut at Texas Station.

A handful of fighters who medaled as amateurs in the Olympics later broke into the pros with fanfare—guys like Mayweather and Sugar Ray Leonard. But that was rare. Most amateurs were 17- or 18-year-old kids whose names would come up on the agenda for the commission to review. I would go down the street to the Golden Gloves Gym, to the Top Rank Gym or to Johnny Tocco's and stand in the corner to watch them spar and workout and. Just about every fighter looks great hitting the bags, but when he gets hit back in the ring, it's a different story. A fighter with seemingly impressive moves might not be able to go four rounds without getting winded. If they couldn't, it was a red flag. We don't want anyone to get hurt because of our own carelessness or assumptions. If they failed my eye test, we often gave them or month or so before they could try again. If you watch enough of a sport, you instinctively can spot the special ones. For decades, I've been running the shot clock for UNLV basketball. I can tell by the way certain freshman or sophomores move, how physical they are and if they might have what it takes to go pro. Guys like Larry Johnson, who led the championship Running Rebels team in 1990 come to mind. Boxing is not much different. Some fighters just have the whole package, almost right away.

The more I watched the amateurs, the more I learned what to look for: the way their feet move, how they block a punch or move along with one that lands. It's amazing how some guys can take a punch better than others and how they turn their hands to increase the impact of their own punches. Every once in a while, I'd laugh to myself: 30 years after paying a dollar to watch Sonny Liston spar on stage at the Thunderbird Hotel, I was in charge of deciding who got to climb into the ring. Life is strange sometimes.

Besides approving the fighters, I also had to approve the fights themselves. Boxing leans heavily, maybe too heavily, on fighters' records. Consequently, every promoter's goal is to have the least approvable opponent for their fighter so that he can get a win. It's always been like that, and it always will be. Promoters have their matchmakers who deal in the details. They study the available opponents, strengths, weaknesses, and probabilities and then come up with the fights. When I was working with a trustworthy matchmaker—one I had a relationship with—it was easier for me to approve the fight. If not, I'd be on my guard. As such, I had to say no a lot more than I said yes, but I learned to disagree without being disagreeable. I had to keep relationships with people, but I was also putting people's lives and livelihoods at stake when I put them in the ring. To this day, I make sure not to forget that.

In boxing, there were always guys who were 25-0 from beating a series of low-caliber opponents. The problem with relying only on records is that they aren't standardized. They mean different things in different places. There was less attention to "strength of schedule," as they call it in college football. The fighters out in Philadelphia, for instance, are far tougher than other places. So, a 10-0 fighter from Tucson might get really hurt by a 5-foot-5 guy from Philly. It was my job to know that, at the same time promoters were trying to make sure I didn't.

One of the more difficult fighters I had to approve match-ups for was Eric Esch, known as Butterbean.[*] Top Rank advertised him as "The King of the Four Rounders." He weighed just under 400 pounds and had no stamina, but if anyone of that size hits you, the damage is serious. As such, he was knocking out guys left and right. It was always hard to get an opponent for him, and I'd have major disagreements finding someone who wouldn't get knocked out the first time one of Eric's punches landed.

On top of everything else, the job of a regulator is to know the fighters—read, study, watch film, and see them in person. Essentially, you're doing all the legwork to cut through the promoters' hype, and there's a lot of it. For any boxer's record to mean anything, there has to be integrity in the system. There were always manipulators trying to get things through. My job was to not let them.

Of course, in Nevada, boxing is not just about sports and entertainment; it's also about gambling. Serious money passes hands before these fights, which adds an extra layer to the importance of making sure everything is fair. The Nevada State Athletic Commission was always under a spotlight, which felt more like a microscope. We knew the gaming commission was looking carefully at what we did, and the public would know if something didn't smell right. More than other sports, we felt the weight of

---

[*] The nickname came from a diet he was forced to go on to lose weight.

that importance because regular people's money was always at stake. Altogether, it added up to a world that needed integrity at its center. I made sure to project that, no matter what got thrown my way. And most everything did.

CHAPTER SIX

■ ■ ■

Iron Age

"Hunger and pride make heavyweight giants."
—Jerry Izenberg[19]

When I read this line, I see Mike Tyson's face. Besides growing up in a similarly difficult childhood, Tyson had some of the Sonny Liston persona in him. He had the scowl. The venom. The eyes that held the desire to destroy. And of course, the legal troubles, which haunted both fighters. Tyson spoke of how he saw Liston in himself—in more ways than one.

"Iron Mike" entered the sport like a hurricane, a juggernaut. In Thomas Hauser's words, "Everyone knew who he was, and everyone had an opinion about him."[20] His reign wasn't as long as we thought it would be, but while it lasted, it was an unforgettable time. In my role at the commission, it sure brought some headaches, as well.

Since beginning as an inspector in 1985, through my time with the commission, into my 14 years at UFC, I've seen countless fighters behind closed doors—rookies to journeymen to veterans. No one warmed up like Tyson. Being in his dressing room before a fight was always a tense experience. I wouldn't even call what Mike did "warming up." Stoking a fire would be a more appropriate phrase.

While Tyson got his hands wrapped, his eyes stared straight ahead, focused into some hole that only he knew how to access. Once his gloves were laced up, it was like a switch had been flipped. His trainer, Richie Giachetti (who once worked with Larry Holmes), held up the big mitts, and Tyson would punch him so hard that he'd lift Richie, who was not a small man, off the ground, sometimes even knocking him back. I'd have to flatten myself up against the concrete wall when Mike started hitting those mitts. Then his entourage would circle around him, rubbing his shoulders, hyping him up, getting him ready to go. Mike knew how to play up his persona. He would be in just a towel over his head or shoulders, black trunks and black shoes. I don't even think he wore socks.

Tyson wanted to break a sweat and be ready before he even walked out. If you watch video of those fights, you can see he's sweating before even entering the ring. By the time the crowd first caught a glimpse of him, he was already mentally inside the fight. During the referee's instructions, you could sense this impatience in his eyes. In his mind, the fight had already started. Cus D'Amato, Tyson's first trainer, told him from a young age that Liston won fights before he ever stepped into the ring, just by intimidating the other fighter. If you watch Tyson's pre-fight demeanor, it is clear he internalized that lesson. He later said, "Most guys lost the fight before they even got hit."[21] It wasn't just talk; he was absolutely right. His ferocity just emanated out in an elemental, almost chemical way, changing the room when he entered.

Tyson was the last fighter D'Amato trained. D'Amato was a legend, a New York guy who had discovered 14-year old Floyd Patterson in his Manhattan gym and built him into a two-time champion. Cus once said he always knew Patterson "lacked the killer instinct,"[22] a problem Tyson certainly did not have. It was no coincidence that Patterson set the record for youngest heavyweight champion in history until the 20-year-old Tyson broke it.

When Mike was a teenager, D'Amato was running a gym in the Catskills, in upstate New York, training a stable of young fighters. Tyson, 12 years old at that time, had been a disciplinary problem back home in Brooklyn and was brought to the attention of D'Amato trainer Teddy Atlas. D'Amato then took over the young phenom and mentored him in things well beyond boxing, becoming his legal guardian and taking him in as one of the family. Cus would train him into one of the most fearsome champions who ever lived.

Mike first appeared on my radar as an idea, a rumor whispered among the boxing community, a legend floating across the country. As an amateur in the 1984 Box-Offs at Caesars Palace for the Olympic boxing team, he was defeated by Henry Tillman in a three-round decision. Amateur fights are not judged or refereed the same as pro fights, so a pure puncher like Mike is hurt by the amateur way of officiating. Once he turned pro, there was word about this kid in New York who was knocking guys out in the first round, and the buzz on him got louder and louder. By then, Don King had gotten behind him, hyping him in his theatrical style. But Tyson was one of the few fighters who fully delivered on the hype.

I remember first laying eyes on Tyson when I was an inspector at his 1986 fight against Alonzo Ratliff at the Las Vegas Hilton, which was stopped in the second round. The next fight was a second-round TKO against Trevor Berbick, which made him the first undisputed heavyweight champion in almost a decade. After that, there was a string of fighters—Pinkland Thomas, Tony Tucker, Frank Bruno, James Smith—all who went down quickly. In my mind, it plays like a "Rocky"-style montage style to a rock-'n'-roll soundtrack.

As someone who has seen hundreds, maybe thousands, of fights, I appreciated how fast Tyson worked. There was no feeling-out period like with most fighters, sizing the other guy up, dancing around the opponent in the early rounds. Tyson's hits were like gunshots to the head—rarely do professional fighters get hit as cleanly as the way he struck them. If you watch those fights, the opponents just look stunned when they went down. In Atlantic City, when Tyson knocked out former champion Michael Spinks in 91 seconds, Spinks just seemed like a scared boy. "Speed kills," D'Amato told his protégé, and Tyson indeed worked fast. Cus, who passed away the year before Tyson became champ, also said that a fighter can't be knocked down by a punch he sees coming. A lot of boxers throw jabs for this very reason: to distract opponents from the follow-up punch that will knock him down.

Another problem Tyson gave other fighters is that his fights were so short that it was hard for opponents to get footage of him to study. It was another way Mike changed the sport; even though his fights were over in a blink, people always tuned in to see him. Having a transcendent heavyweight like that energizes the whole sport. (Nowadays, Deontay Wilder has that same one-punch ability.) Word traveled fast that you just had to see this guy. Heavyweight fights are different because their punches are that much harder. When people paid to see a Tyson fight, they knew it might be over in a blink. It got to the point where that was the *expectation*.

Tyson was a strange mix. He was shorter than other heavyweights at 5-foot-9 but built like a tank with a gap in his front teeth. His high-pitched lispy voice seemed out of place. Underneath the persona, and especially one-on-one, Tyson was a sweet kid, respectful, and polite. He had a sensitive side that would come out after the fight or when talking about the late D'Amato, his beloved father figure. I remember taking my young kids to school one day when we saw Mike running alongside a park. I pulled up next to him, and he stopped to say hi to the kids, which was not something other fighters would do. He called me "Mr. Rathner," his lisp dragging the "T" sound with his tongue. He has a big heart, which not everyone knew. Back in those days, immediately after a victory, Mike would run over to the corner, put his arms around the fighter and sometimes kiss him on the cheek.

Boxing may look straightforward—two guys wailing on each other—but it's both an art and a science. Obviously, the goal is to hit (and to not be hit), and both are happening near simultaneously. This means you have to be defensive in your offense. Some fighters know they can take a punch and just trust they can land enough of their own to hurt the other guy. Their defense strategy is tiring the other guy out, knowing they'll be standing at the end. That was the idea behind Ali's rope-a-dope strategy. It's why conditioning is so essential, even more so than other sports. Because of the footwork, the strategy, the ways to get inside, the methods for blocking or moving with punches, you have to have a game plan. But Tyson made that difficult, forcing opponents just to try to stay standing. "Everybody has a plan until they get punched in the mouth," he famously said.

And it finally happened to him, too.

In February 1990, James "Buster" Douglas literally shocked the world when he knocked out Tyson as a 42-to-1 underdog in Tokyo. (That's an overused phrase, but this time it was true.) Tyson was not himself that night, sluggish and slow, moving "like a man trying to cross a mud puddle while wearing snowshoes" in Jerry Izenberg's colorful words.[23] I wasn't in either fighters' dressing room that night, but if I had been, I'm sure I would've seen the signs of what was to come. Word was that Tyson was having personal problems. We all knew he was in midst of a divorce, and more than few observers felt he wasn't focused on his training. The week of the fight, he had apparently been out partying every night in Tokyo and a sparring partner had even knocked him down, which no actual opponent had even done.

In hindsight, it's not surprising that an uppercut followed by a combination in the tenth round from Douglas knocked Tyson down and out. But in the moment, it was an absolute stunning development. No one thought Mike could be beat, let alone to lose like that, fumbling on the ground looking for his mouthpiece. It was shocking. Tyson had clearly gotten distracted by the trappings of his fame and the attention that came from being such a visible champion. It's interesting that the same thing happened to Douglas soon after, and in a much more compressed period of time.

Douglas' next fight, as champion, was against Evander Holyfield. Holyfield was an Olympic medalist and devout Christian who would unfairly spend much of his career in Tyson's shadow. However, drawing Douglas at that moment was fortuitous. In the intervening eight months since Douglas became champion, he had gained 26 pounds, ballooning to 246. Even his cornermen were surprised when he stepped on the scales. I remember that weigh-in so well. Right after Douglas weighed in, there was a mass exodus of gamblers making a mad dash to the sportsbook to bet against him. They would've doubled their bets if they had seen what I saw before the fight.[24]

I was in Douglas' dressing room at the Mirage in the hours beforehand, and it was obvious to me he was in trouble. He was sitting on a table, waiting for a ride or something, just drained of energy. It was obvious that he hadn't trained well and he wasn't in good shape. I almost felt bad for him. Here was the heavyweight champion of the world, and I got the feeling he didn't stand a chance. Word around town was that he was eating pizza in the sauna. Before the fight, I told one of the commissioners that either Douglas was "one of the most confident guys I've ever seen or he is no way ready to fight."

The answer came soon enough. Douglas lost before he ever stepped into the ring. Holyfield embarrassed him. Actually, it'd be more accurate to say Douglas embarrassed himself. Unlike most other sports, there is absolutely no way to hide in a boxing match. Both Tyson's and Douglas' knockouts remind me of the Joe Frazier line, "If you cheated in the dark of the morning, you're getting found out now under the bright lights."

Maybe the whole significance of being the heavyweight champion got to Douglas, or maybe he just didn't have the discipline to sustain it. Knocking out Tyson was an unbelievable feat. He had pulled off the biggest upset in boxing history, but he just didn't handle it well. I don't care what anyone assumes; it's not easy being the champ, even for eight months. I've known a lot of champs in my lifetime, and it's a tough position to be in. Everyone simultaneously loves you, wants things from you, and is gunning for you. As the saying goes, "Uneasy lies the head that wears a crown." Tyson understood how a thing like that could happen. I don't know if the two of them ever talked about it.

CHAPTER SEVEN

■ ■ ■

Tyson's Return and 'Bite Night'

"Boxers were liars. Champions were great liars. They had to be. Once you knew what they thought, you could hit them. So, their personalities became masterpieces of concealment."

—Norman Mailer[25]

> Dear Marc:
>
> I appreciate every consideration you have given me here in Nevada. I am working hard to honor my commitment to you. I am presently training at the Golden Gloves Gym and I would be pleased to thank you in person if you stop by.
>
> Wishing you a joyous Holiday Season,
>
> Mike Tyson

A Holiday Card from Mike Tyson.

In my opinion, rarely has a sport been dictated—for good and for ill—for so long by one man. Maybe Michael Jordan in the '90s, but there's no other competition for Tyson's impact on boxing. Mike was like a shot of adrenaline for the entire sport that was mostly positive until the bottom fell out. In 1992, Tyson was convicted of sexual assault (a charge he denied) and sent to prison for three years. Because of the nature of Tyson's impact on boxing, his absence left a gigantic hole. During those years, it felt like the heavyweight division, and thus all of boxing, was on hiatus.

After Tyson's early release in the spring of 1995, he immediately signed an exclusive and lucrative deal with Don King, who made it clear Mike was ready to fight again. The challenge for the matchmakers was to figure out who should be his opponent. It was hard for the commission as well. We had no idea what kind of shape Tyson was in or what prison had done to affect his fighting, either psychologically or physically. It had been four years since his last fight, so everything was just a big question mark. How do you approve a fight with such a huge variable—especially with someone as fiercely talented and unpredictable as Mike Tyson?

While the promoters are out selling fights, their matchmakers have to put fighters up against each other. A good one, like Bruce Trampler—who matched up everyone from to De La Hoya to Mayweather—knows how to pace the fighters' career, how to match them against the right guys, and how to build up their records while also ensuring they're prepared. If not, the fighters would get their clocks cleaned by a hungry, ambitious fighter.

There's no real parallel in any other sport. Nowhere else can someone pick and choose opponents—design a career, really—the way you can in boxing. In team sports, you play who's on the schedule. In individual sports like golf and tennis, the opponents revolve around the big tournaments. Meanwhile, you have mediocre fighters in boxing with astounding records; thus, promoters and matchmakers play a huge part in the sport at large. The records can be easily fixed. In my opinion, the lack of standardization hurts the sport. What does 20-1 even mean in that environment? I wasn't even sure, even though it was literally my job to be in charge of such things.

So, in the spring of 1995, the commission had to approve Tyson's first post-prison match, working off very little information. King's matchmaker proposed Peter McNeely, a Boston fighter and former Marine who was 36-1 off a pretty unimpressive collection of East Coast opponents. His record was manipulated past the point of realism, but we figured it evened out against an opponent who had been behind bars for three years and hadn't fought for four. To be honest, we were rolling the dice. I just said, "Let's see what happens."

The night of the fight, there was a buzzing all over the Strip. Celebrities, gamblers, athletes, and fight fans all flooded in. Tyson's return was an event. The MGM Grand—which had signed an exclusive deal with King and Tyson—was packed with the crowd at peak volume. McNeely wasn't even on the fight poster. It was only a menacing picture of Mike and the tagline: "He's Back." What more did you need?

Right at the opening bell, McNeely was all sloppy adrenaline, charging across the ring to throw random punches at Tyson. It took Mike about eight seconds to hit him with a right and knock him down. McNeely popped up immediately and started circling around the ring. Referee Mills Lane had to grab Pete by the arm to give him the mandatory eight count. McNeely got a few more shots in, but once Tyson found his rhythm and hit him with a few combinations, that was it. Sixty seconds later, he was down again. When McNeely got up a second time, ready to go, McNeely's manager, a Boston guy named Vinny Vecchione, stunned everyone by jumping into the ring to stop the fight.

The crowd was upset, the TV guys were upset, and I was upset, too. Everyone wants to see a fight come to its natural conclusion. McNeely was able to defend himself, and Vinny's response was totally uncalled for. I said so in the press. It was rare for me to make a case like that in the newspapers, but I was angry. It took away from Tyson's return and overshadowed the fight with unneeded controversy, one of the few involving Tyson that didn't come from Mike himself. It also looked bad. Considering the heightened build-up, the whole sport of boxing ended up looking like a shady money grab. What angered me the most was that, in defending his actions, Vinny referenced the fighter Jimmy Garcia, who was killed earlier that year during a fight. The comparison was insulting. That was a long fight, 11 rounds, which was ultimately stopped and put Garcia into a nearly two-week coma before he passed.

The commission held onto Vecchione's share of the purse for a week to ensure there was no evidence of wrongdoing, such as betting on Tyson in the first round. In the end, the gaming commission found nothing. Vecchione became infamous, and McNeely got 15 minutes of fame and cast in a Pizza Hut commercial, all for getting hit a few times by Tyson. It was nowhere near a satisfying conclusion, but Iron Mike was back—or so we thought.

Me (bottom left) keeping Frank Bruno from falling through the ropes after a punch from Tyson. You can see referee Mills Lane making sure Tyson doesn't hit him again.
Photo courtesy Mike Nelson/AFP via Getty Images.

A few months later, Tyson won a three-round TKO against gigantic Englishman Frank Bruno for the lineal heavyweight belt. As Mills Lane waved off the fight, Bruno had lost his balance from the barrage of punches. I instinctively stood up and put my hands out to prevent his 250 pounds from falling through the ropes. You just don't forget a thing like that. The same thing happened a few years earlier in a Bowe-Holyfield fight.

In September 1996, Tyson embarrassed Bruce Seldon in a fight that lasted fewer than two minutes. In the ring, Tyson ate up all the space between themm and Seldon went down in the first round after Tyson grazed him on the top of his head. Seldon got up, but after a left hook from Tyson, he went down again and was wobbly on his feet. That was it. It was one of the shortest heavyweight title fights in history.*

All of these fights were a preamble for a Tyson-Evander Holyfield match-up, which was nearly a decade in the making. The two fighters knew each other from their amateur days. (In the 1984 Olympic trials, Holyfield made the team, but Tyson did not). It was set to happen in 1991, but the Buster Douglas fight and a Tyson rib injury put it on hold. Then Tyson went away.

By 1996, Evander was 34 years old, with recent heart problems. In a fight against Bobby Czyz, he looked tepid, barely eking out a win. He looked like a shell of himself, and some felt that Tyson's team jumped on the chance for him to fight an underwhelming Holyfield. In fact, the commission was unsure about Holyfield's fitness to fight and mandated that he go up to the Mayo Clinic for a battery of tests, where he was given a clean bill of health.

"Finally," the fight was billed. Then, in a typical understated fashion, King said at the press conference that nearly half the world would watch the fight. "Every barbershop, every restaurant, every cab driver, every *lumpenproletariat*** to the elitest—presidents, kings,

---

* That fight was notable as the one attended by rapper Tupac Shakur before his fatal shooting hours later.

** This is a Marxist term that I had to look up.

dictators are all interested in the fight," King proclaimed in his distinctive erudition.

After opening as a 25-to-1 underdog, Holyfield was 6-to-1 on fight night in November 1996. Tyson came out strong from the outset, but Holyfield didn't back down, which I think changed the tenor of the fight. Mike was used to almost bullying opponents into submission. At the end of the first round, Tyson hit Holyfield right after the bell and Holyfield retaliated, showing him he wouldn't allow it. It was a sign of things to come. For the rest of the fight, Holyfield mostly took control, even knocking down a stunned Tyson, something that had only happened one time in Mike's career. The crowd, which was probably more in Tyson's camp at the outset, shifted enmass to the challenger's side, chanting "*Holy-field, Holy-field.*" In the tenth round, Holyfield decimated Tyson, pounding away on him at will, but Mike wouldn't go down. When the bell rang, I wasn't even sure Mike would be out for the eleventh round. Then early in the next round, when it was clear Holyfield was having his way, the referee—Mitch Halpern—stopped the fight. The crowd went ballistic in excitement.

There are no rules in Nevada against betting for your own guy, and Holyfield's camp made off like bandits that night. Lou Duva, Tommy Brooks and the rest of his team had so much faith that they bet big on Evander. With those odds, it was a healthy chunk of change they took home. Before we even hit the exits that night, we knew we'd be prepping for the next one. Seven months later, in June 1997, the rematch was going to land like a missile.

Selecting the officials is part of the commission's job, though it rarely gets much attention. Because of what had happened in the first fight and what would eventually happen in the rematch, the officials became hotly debated—through no fault of their own. Mitch Halpern, a young guy had trained under the legendary Richard Steele, did a stellar job in the first fight, which was a hectic and action-packed match. He stopped it at the perfect time and didn't become the focus, as some referees tend to do. The commission was more than happy to put him forward again, but Tyson's camp objected. In those days, Tyson was represented by John Horn and Rory Holloway, a friend from his Catskills boxing days. Don King paid them to visit Mike in prison every week, and he signed with them while he was in there. In a commission meeting less than a week before the fight, Horn and Holloway—with King at their side—levied a protest against Halpern working the rematch. The complaint was that Halpern didn't stop Evander from leading with his head. There were some vague threats from Tyson's camp about him dropping out, but that seemed unlikely, so the commissioners ruled against the protest.

The Tyson camp lobbied for Richard Steele, but fighters don't get to choose their officials. We usually put together a list of judges and referees and listened for any issues they might have. These types of protests weren't unprecedented. George Foreman once protested Mills Lane working his fight because Mills had criticized him during an HBO broadcast. It was a $10,000 fee for Mitch, a high-profile fight, and the commission felt he had earned it. He and I talked several times that week, and I tried to feel him out. "If you feel that the pressure with them complaining is going to bother you," I said, "then we can…"

"No, it's fine," he said. "I can handle it."

The Tyson-Holyfield rematch was front-page sports news all week, and the conflict over Halpern got a lot of ink. Two days before the fight, Mitch called me. "You know, Marc, I shouldn't be the focus of the fight. I shouldn't be the story. It's not fair to the fighters. I'm not going to accept the fight." It was a classy move and exactly the thing a natural official would say. It made me respect him even more. Dropping out turned out to be a fortuitous decision.

After Mitch bowed out, the commission had about 24 hours to agree on Mills Lane and fly him in from Reno. Mills was a character, an older guy with a high-pitched Southern drawl he got growing up on his well-to-do family's plantation. He was a Marine and former NCAA welterweight champion before going to law school to become a district attorney and then a judge. I liked Mills, who usually came in the night before the fight and would play poker at one of the hotels. He was a classic by-the-book guy, and not just in the ring. In his courtroom, if an attorney was even one minute late, he would dismiss their case. He had no time for nonsense. And he was about to get a handful.

There was an enormous crowd for the weigh-in that Friday afternoon, and I got a rush of nervous excitement while weighing the fighters. I was always a behind-the-scenes guy, but Tyson-Holyfield was a thrill for me—a mega event. The weigh-in was covered from reporters and fans from all over the world.

The night of the fight I took a circuitous route through the MGM Grand's bars, shops, and hallways to get a look around. There was an inordinate number of people out and about—many hours before the fight. When I arrived at the arena, empty with exception of the officials and television crews, I went through my regular routine. I checked in on the inspectors and met with the officials to hand out the assignments for the night's fights. "This is going to be a fun night," I told them. "It's a great time to be part of boxing."

I then measured and walked the ring to make sure the canvas was smooth all the way around and tested the tension of the ropes to make sure they weren't loose. As Executive Director of the commission, I felt as though I was the sturdy bottom to make sure fights went off without a hitch. Everything wasn't necessarily my responsibility, but if something went wrong, I felt like it was my fault. I always carried different colored boxing shorts in the trunk of my car and extra gloves of all sizes. A small detail could bring the show to a crashing halt. I thought of myself as the goalkeeper who couldn't let anything pass through. You never knew what could happen, so I liked to be prepared. But there was no way I could've been prepared for what went down that night.

By the time of the main event, everyone was at a fever pitch. The lights dimmed, the fighters and camps poured out of the tunnels, Jimmy Lennon Jr. bellowed his introduction, the fighters stared each other down, and then Mills delivered his trademark phrase, "Let's get it on!"

After a solid, if forgettable, first round, things started to slide off the rails. Holyfield was leading with his head again, which opened a cut above Tyson's right eye that Mills ruled as an accidental headbutt. Part of my job was notifying the judges and TV broadcast of the ruling with a two-way sign: "Cut caused by an accidental headbutt" on one side and "Cut caused by a punch" on the other.* By the end of the second round, there had been a lot of incidental contact between the fighters, and Evander's head butting was making Tyson upset. Mike was so ready to go at the start of the third round that he came out without his mouthguard. Mills spotted it immediately and sent him back to Richie Giachetti to put it in. I don't think that had anything to do with what happened next, though there would be theories about it for years afterward.

The third round was messy, with lots of clinches and separations, leading to a moment of stoppage late in the round. After separating Holyfield and Tyson, Mills called timeout after Mike's mouthguard fell into the ring. Just then, Evander jumped up and down and spun around. I was sitting right there with my hands on the apron, but I didn't know what had happened. I thought maybe Tyson kneed him or his cup pinched him, but Holyfield was holding his glove by his face. Mills sent both fighters to their corners, and the doctor, Flip Homansky, came in to look at Holyfield. Holyfield's corner showed Mills what had happened. Tyson had bitten off a piece of Holyfield's right ear! Then Mills gestured for me to come up onto the apron. I think the people watching on television had more of a sense of what was going on. The replay clearly showed the bite, but at the arena, there was no way of knowing.

Mills approached me. "He's disqualified," he said. "He bit his ear. He's out."

"What happened?" I asked, still processing it all.

---

* If a fight is stopped from bleeding from a punch, that's a TKO. But if a cut from a headbutt stops a fight, it could be a technical decision or a no-contest, depending on when it happens.

"He bit his ear! I can see the bite mark."

"Ok," I said calmly. "Are you sure you want to disqualify him?" I wasn't doubting Mills' decision. It was just my instincts kicking in from years of being an official. My goal was not to question the decision. It was to get Mills to take a beat to be sure of what he was doing. It had nothing to do with the millions watching or the attention on the fight. It was just my automatic response. I didn't overrule him at all; Mills later said my question "brought me back to my senses." In all sports, it's a big decision to eject someone—especially when it ends the match, as it does in boxing. You don't want to determine the outcome like that.

Right after I asked Mills if he was sure, he realized he shouldn't be too hasty. He took a second and said, "Let me ask the doctor." He then walked over to Flip, asking if Holyfield could go on. Once he got the okay, Mills deducted two points from Tyson: one for the bite and one for pushing Holyfield after timeout was called.

After Mills spoke to Tyson's corner, Mike weakly protested, "That's from a punch."

"That's bullshit!" Mills replied. Even a Tyson punch couldn't knock part of a guy's ear off. I was right there and made sure Giachetti understood his fighter had been warned. It made what happened next all the more shocking.

The final 30 seconds of the third round finished after more jostling between the fighters. By the time the bell rang, I was poking my head through ropes, screaming to the judges about the original two-point penalty when Mills approached me. He said that Tyson was disqualified for a second bite. *A second bite!?* It was just chaos after that. Holyfield had every reason to be livid—he was bleeding from both ears, one of which had a piece missing—and yet did an admirable job keeping his cool. After Mills disqualified him, Tyson did not do the same.

By that point, I was standing outside the ropes on the apron. All of a sudden, people from both camps came flooding into the ring. They were mostly meandering around until Tyson tried to get at

Holyfield. Then inspectors, commission officials, arena security, and Las Vegas police swarmed in. It was just a mass of maybe 50 people in the ring, and at the center of it, the eye of the storm, was Mike swinging at anyone within range. After a brief respite, Tyson started up again and had to be restrained from going after Holyfield. The crowd's boos were deafening, their dissatisfaction only matched by their confusion.

I didn't climb into the ring at that point. What could I do? This thing was running well past my control. Our job was going to be to clean up the mess. When the fighters left the ring, the crowd started getting downright unruly, and you could sense it was spilling into the hotel and casino, where a riot broke out. At one point, people thought they'd heard gunshots. As I was hustled out a side entrance by a security guard into the chaotic Las Vegas night, I knew my job was just beginning.

Teddy Atlas, who knew Tyson from a young age, speculated that the bites were Tyson's way of getting out of a fight he knew he couldn't win. I'm not so sure. It's hard to get inside a person's head, and Mike didn't strike me as someone who reacted with pre-meditation. He was a pretty impulsive guy, especially back then. There was a press conference that night around midnight at which the commission had to face the public. We said we'd be holding Tyson's purse and we'd investigate—watch film of the fight and figure out the appropriate response.

I knew I was going to have a horrible Monday.

Two days later, Mike stood at a podium in an off-white suit and read a statement that was clearly written by a public relations professional—hitting all the right notes but not sounding much like himself. (It was actually written by my old friend Sig Rogich, whom King contacted to help manage the media fallout.) Calls bombarded my office from every type of media outlet, and because I made a point of trying to answer every one, it was a madhouse.

The second bite showed Tyson had really lost it, but it also saved both Mills and me from scrutiny. If Mike would've knocked Holyfield out after the first bite, there would've been all kinds of questions about Mills (and by extension, my) letting the fight go on. But Evander did note (in his memoir) that he didn't blame me for questioning the initial decision. As for Mills, he had always been a respected judge and a character in Las Vegas and boxing circles, but the "Bite Fight" turned him into a national celebrity. He wrote a book, starred in a cartoon show, "Celebrity Deathmatch," and a reality show called "Judge Mills Lane." Announcer Steve Albert and Jim Gray also lifted their profiles because of their coverage during that fight. Gray's post-fight interviews with Mills, Holyfield, Tyson, his manager John Horne, and even Don King, catapulted him to broadcast fame.

The Nevada State Athletic Commission met that week to uphold the original suspension. A week later, we had a public hearing in chambers at Las Vegas City Hall. The media came out in force for that one: live feeds, antenna farms and satellite trucks on the streets blocking the building. It was a public meeting, but there was so much press that I'm not sure how much of the public got in. I was there with the five commissioners, the deputy attorney general, Tyson's lawyer Oscar Goodman, and some of Mike's other representatives for an open debate discussing Tyson's punishment. Artist Leroy Neiman was among the crowd, and afterward, he sent me a nice letter and portrait he sketched on the back of the agenda—a souvenir from an incredibly hectic period. By unanimous decision, the commission revoked Tyson's boxing license (he could re-apply in a year) and fined him 10 percent of his purse ($3 million), which at the time, I believe, was the largest individual fine in sports history. I spoke to Mitch Halpern a few days after the fight, and we talked about what might have been.

"Boy, you sure made the right decision on this one," I told him.

"I know it," he said, sounding relieved. "You're right."

"You would have gotten the blame. Tyson's camp would've said, "We told you we didn't want him!" We had a small laugh about the controversy that he dodged.

That was the beginning of the end for Tyson. He was never really the same in the ring after that, and we all knew it. The "Bite Fight" was a bizarre and unprecedented moment in boxing history, in cultural history actually, but it was also the turning point for Mike. "It's easy to do anything in victory," Floyd Patterson once said. "It's in defeat that a man reveals himself."[26]

Observing referee Mills Lane warn Tyson after the first bite. Though the ring card girl is holding Round 4, it was actually the middle of Round 3.

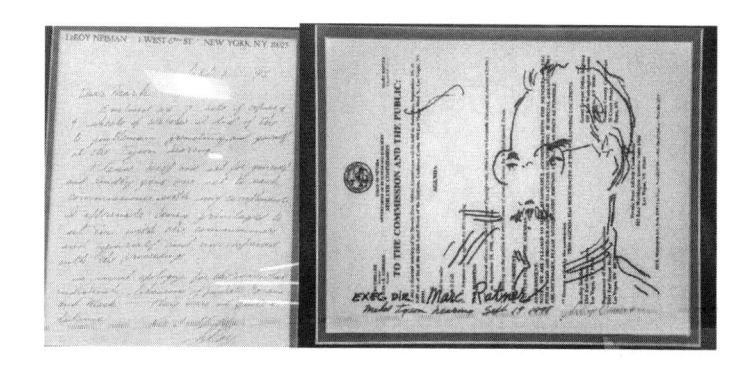

A note and sketch of me from artist Leroy Neiman who observed the Tyson bite hearing at Las Vegas City Hall.

CHAPTER EIGHT

■ ■ ■

The Bizarre and the Tragic

"Boxing is the theater of the unexpected."

—Larry Merchant

"May you live in interesting times," the old English saying goes. I had the great fortune of running the commission at the apex of "interesting" in boxing. Tyson was certainly around for some of the most bizarre and controversial moments of my career, including the "Bite Fight," but he wasn't there for the absolute strangest. That happened on the night of November 6, 1993.

At the fights, my seat was always in the same place: front row, facing the camera, to the right of one of the judges on an elevated bar stool. It was surreal to see famous athletes or movie stars taking seats behind me. Here's what I remember from that night. During the seventh round of the Holyfield-Riddick Bowe title fight outdoors at Caesars Palace, there was a feeling that the crowd's attention had been pulled elsewhere. It often meant that a fight had broken out somewhere in the stands. There was a rumbling, like a collective murmuring, and a feeling that the energy was being pulled away from the ring.

I didn't hear any strange noises, nor did I look up. My job was to focus on the fight, so that's where my attention stayed. Some later reported that they saw a figure gliding around in the sky above Caesars Palace, but I had no advanced warning whatsoever. For me, it was immediate. Out of the darkness, a man hooked to a giant contraption landed on the ropes in Bowe's corner. I jumped up in shock, as many did. Wearing a red jumpsuit and white helmet, the man was attached to wires, and a parachute that had gotten tangled in the overhead lights, his body wrapped up in the ring's ropes. He could've pulled down some heavy equipment, and he was lucky no one was hurt.

Promptly dragged down from the canvas by security and the guys in Bowe's corner, the guy found himself surrounded by a surprised and angry crowd.* Marion Barry and Louis Farrakhan were in that section, and the burly Nation of Islam bodyguards really went at this guy, and I caught a glimpse of them ramming him with their big brick cellphones. The "Fan Man," as he was later named for his distinctive propellers, had just ambushed a heavyweight title fight. It wasn't anywhere in the rule book, and it didn't have any comparable precedent. We were, no pun intended, flying blind.

During the chaos, while everyone pushed and craned to get a good look at the madness, I was probably the only one in the arena not paying attention to the melee. There was still a fight going on, so my officiating instincts kicked in. First, I ran over to the timekeeper to mark how much time was left. Then I ran over to each judge and told them the same thing. "This fight may not continue," I yelled above the noise. "On the back of your scorecard make a note of where you are!" People forget that the memorable interruption overshadowed

---

* In a post-9/11 world, the immediate reaction would have been to be much more terrified. At the time, it seemed mostly like a goofy stunt.

what had been a pretty amazing heavyweight title fight. It had been a real puncher's duel up to that point.

During the commotion, I got up into the ring, as police swarmed in, and spoke to Mills Lane about how to proceed. He handled it like the pro that he is, and I give enormous credit to ring announcer Michael Buffer who did a stellar job keeping the crowd calm during a situation that could've caused panic. If the same "Fan Man" incident happened in 2003 instead of 1993, we'd have thought it was a terrorist attack.

There was one error I made that night that still bothers me. During the break, the fighters just sat in their corners, with Bowe's team using the time to fix up his cuts. In retrospect, I should've sent Holyfield and Bowe back to their respective dressing rooms during the delay, which ended up being 21 minutes long. They were just sitting outside in their shorts with jackets draped over them, the sweat getting cold on their bodies in the November night air. (Bowe's wife, who was pregnant, actually fainted and was taken to the hospital, though she ended up being fine.) As for the "Fan Man," he was taken away by Las Vegas Police, charged and released on $200 bail, his place securely written in the history books for causing the weirdest sports interruption in history.

The fight eventually resumed, with Holyfield winning the title by the narrowest decision—one point. The interrupted seventh round was scored completely evenly: one judge had it 10-9 Bowe, another had it 10-9 for Holyfield, and the third had it even. If the third judge had scored the round for Bowe 10-9, then the decision would have been a majority draw and Bowe would have kept the title. Something people still don't think about: Was it because of all the hoopla with the interruption that changed the fight's course, which then changed heavyweight boxing history?

The "Fan Man" got folk-hero status, and the incident regularly tops lists of the strangest things ever to happen during a sporting event. Bowe has been quoted saying it was all a conspiracy to help Holyfield, but I just don't see how that can be argued in good faith.

Bowe was probably annoyed, as he had a right to be. The rest of us got one of the strangest memories of our lives.

■ ■ ■

There have been tragedies in boxing, and it would be unfair of me to avoid discussing them. They came with the job, and they are part of the sport's history just as much as the victories. Tommy Morrison was a former WBO heavyweight champion, a big-name fighter (he co-starred in "Rocky V") on a path to an eventual showdown with Mike Tyson. Before a February 1996 fight in Las Vegas against Arthur "Stormy" Weathers, the 27-year-old Morrison had to take a blood test—for HIV and hepatitis—to be licensed in the state. At first, Morrison refused on religious grounds, but when I told him he couldn't fight otherwise, he reluctantly agreed. We were the only state that tested for HIV at the time, and we had been doing so since Chuck Minker's reign. In a sport where blood, cuts, and open wounds are prevalent, it just made sense. While other sports dragged their feet, we jumped on taking the precaution. As I mentioned, Chairman Dr. Ghanem was instrumental in making sure of this.

The afternoon of the Morrison-Weathers fight, I got a call from Dr. Ghanem, giving me the news that Tommy had tested positive for HIV. It was a shock, to say the least, but I didn't even have time to sit with it. I had to break the news to his camp that the fight was off. I went to Tony Holden, Morrison's manager, in his suite to give him the news about the canceled fight. I didn't mention HIV specifically; I really should not have been the one bringing the news of such a personal and medical nature. All I said was that Tommy couldn't be licensed for the night's fight, and that he should talk to his doctor back in Oklahoma. To this day, I wish that a medical professional had been selected to break the news.

Steve Albert interviewed me on Showtime that night and tried to get me to reveal more, but the state's attorney general made it very clear what I was and wasn't allowed to say. Morrison didn't pass the medical tests and thus didn't meet licensing requirements. I was overly cautious about saying one word more. Though I understood the curiosity—a major fight had been canceled at the last minute—a man's medical privacy is not my business to offer on national television. When Albert pushed about the suspension, I explained that Morrison "would be suspended worldwide" but would go no further. A few days later, Tommy himself publicly admitted to his diagnosis in a press conference. He did fight once more in Japan later that year, but for all intents and purposes, his fighting career was over.*

The Morrison case became an ongoing controversy because Tommy later claimed the test was inaccurate. After he passed away in 2013, his widow sued the lab and the Nevada State Athletic Commission (naming me personally in the lawsuit) for $100 million. Her claim was that we couldn't prove he had HIV, though the test had 99 percent accuracy and he admitted it himself before pulling back. She's still fighting us on appeal, trying to take the suit to the Nevada Supreme Court. I'm not sure of the motivation but I feel for her. She lost her husband, who had his career taken from him during his prime and his life taken from him at the young age of 44. Still, neither I nor the commission handled the matter improperly at all.

When I first started out as Executive Director, my big worry was just getting to the fight. *Just get to that first bell,* I'd think. After the opening bell and the fighters came out, I felt this enormous sense of relief, like a release. The fight had gone off without a hitch. But of course, that wasn't true. As I got more involved in the job, I realized getting to that point was just the start. The fighters' health and safety were always at risk and their well-being became my preeminent concern. The fight wasn't over until both men walked out of there on their own two feet. Sadly, it didn't always happen.

In my 14 years as Executive Director, seven fighters died in Nevada from injuries sustained in the ring. Each one of those deaths was

---

* One positive development in the whole situation was that HIV testing became far more common across the sport after the Morrison test became public.

devastating, and having to face the fighters' families brought home to me how painful and shocking the loss was. It's the nature of combat sports—whether it's boxing or MMA—that people are getting hit and they can get hurt. We worked extremely hard at providing the utmost safety for the fighters, but these tragedies still happen. Sometimes a fighter would actually walk out of the ring and seem fine, but then some shift happened where they fell or threw up, and they got rushed to the hospital. No matter how glorifying the fights are, those moments will never leave me. It's a part of boxing that isn't seen by everyone, and most fans don't even want to think about it. But it was always part of my job. Each one of those deaths has haunted me.

I remember Jimmy Garcia dying in the hospital after a fight in 1995 against Gabriel Ruelas. We rushed Jimmy immediately to the hospital, got him onto the operating table as fast as humanly possible, but he fell into a coma and died 13 days later. It was a devastating loss. In 2005, my final full year at the commission, a former IBF lightweight champion named Leavander Johnson went into the hospital with a subdural hematoma after a fight against Jesus Chavez. It was not a situation where he took a prolonged beating or the referee had taken too long to stop it. Chavez was not a particularly heavy puncher, and I don't remember a lot of concern at the time. In the eleventh round, Chavez was hitting Johnson with a string of undefended punches, so the referee stepped in and ended it. Johnson actually left the ring on his own, only to collapse later in his dressing room. I remember going to the hospital every day to see how he was doing and sitting with his family. The doctors would tell me, "He's getting better. The swelling is down." I really thought he was going to survive. That Thursday, I walked into the hospital to meet with the family. His cornermen had found out that he had passed away that afternoon, which was among the most difficult experiences I've had in all my years, personally or professionally.

When fighters pass away after a fight, it's possible that the fight is not the sole cause, but an aggravating cause on top of an earlier injury. They may have been knocked out in their training, which contributes to the injury. The problem is we can never really prove that and there's little incentive for the camp to report such a thing. That's one of the issues in the sport. When there's a big championship fight, with serious money on the line, if a guy gets knocked down or knocked out by his sparring partner, it's kept secret from everyone—especially the commission. If we ever did find, it would be months later, long after it mattered. The doctors ask the fighters and the camps these questions at the weigh-in, but it's hard to get an honest answer in that forum. If there was a solid rumor from someone I trusted, we could order an MRI before the fight, but otherwise it's a roll of the dice. I'd love to see that rectified going forward. These are people's lives on the line. Any time I was involved in licensing decisions, and to this day with UFC, I bring the same somberness, attention, and care to making sure the fighter's health and safety is paramount. The sport won't work any other way.

CHAPTER NINE

■ ■ ■

Money and Mayhem

"When [boxing] falls short of perfection, which is almost always, the failures are interesting in themselves. Horrifying or hilarious, and all points in between, no two fights are alike. What happens in and around that mislabeled ring is a potent distillation of everything human."

—Katherine Dunn.[27]

Boxing has long been a part of American popular culture. The country's best writers once congregated around fights, befriended fighters, and wrote up long missives about the drama and glory of boxing. Even though that's no longer the case—team sports now occupy center stage—there's still a symbiotic relationship with the media and writers that is special in boxing.

As Executive Director of the Nevada State Athletic Commission, my phone never stopped ringing. The state had a public relations office, but everyone wanted to hear from me. I was essentially the face and voice of the commission. I learned from the very beginning that I didn't have to go out and get interviews; they all were going to come to me. I wasn't a natural by any stretch of the imagination, but part of my job was to learn how to talk on television, do radio interviews, release statements to the press, and to be interviewed by reporters. These things were integral to the job, so I never ran from it. Back when I worked at R&R Advertising, before I even got into boxing, I got to watch Sig Rogich handle the media with admirable aplomb. Sig was well-read and a politician in his own right. (He worked as a media advisor for President George H.W. Bush). He could answer just about any question with the ideal sound bite. He had this natural gift for it, and I tried to pick up what I could. At the commission, I always made myself available to anyone who contacted me. I actually made a rule for myself, and I made sure my staff knew about it. I never wanted to hear or read, "Ratner was unavailable for comment." My epitaph could be: *he always called back.*

Even if I couldn't answer the question directly, and sometimes I had to stay mum on a certain issue, I'd always return every journalist's call. We'd also get a fair number of calls from fans, sometimes with nasty messages about how inept I or the commission was:

What's wrong with you, Ratner?
How did Mosley get the decision over De La Hoya?
Why don't you throw Tyson out for good this time?

If they left their phone numbers, I would actually call them back. They were always pretty surprised to hear from me. They'd pick up and I'd say, "This is Marc Ratner calling from the Nevada State Athletic Commission. I got your message and let me explain to you. In our opinion..." I got a kick catching them off guard. Even the ones who left the most vicious messages would engage in a conversation with me. There shouldn't be too much distance from the people who run the sport and the fans. If one can have a conversation with the other, than that's a pretty good sign.

With "The Greatest," holding the 1963 picture of me posing with Liston.

I'm an easygoing person, so I think that helped. I'd like to think the boxing world would say I was even-keeled. I didn't get overly excited under pressure and handled whatever came up in a straightforward but amenable way. I made decisions, as I had to do, but was never forceful or obnoxious about it. Having a background as a sports official was immensely helpful. I understood the need to be invisible, to an extent, but *never absent*. That's the key.

After every card, we would have a meeting with the officials to go over the fights to discuss what had happened that night. I would ask the judges to articulate what score they gave, especially if it was far off from the others. If their rationale didn't fit, I might tell them in a private meeting or in my office, "I can't give you a main event at the moment. Concentrate on these four-rounders, these six-rounders, and we'll work you back up to main events." I wouldn't embarrass or chastise them. That doesn't make anyone better at their job.

I tried to communicate without being disrespectful, which was something I picked up during my own time refereeing college football. After every game, there was a post-game review, and a supervisor would come in and yell something like, "Hey Ratner! How the f*** did you miss that clip right in front of you?!" These chew outs would be in front of the whole crew, and it was embarrassing. If you were defensive about it, that just made it worse, so you just had to cower and say you didn't see it. Otherwise, it looked like you didn't know what you were doing. I made a point of being firm but never addressing officials in that manner.

My position at the commission gave me a great deal of perks, which I've enjoyed. I had the rare and strange opportunity to play myself in two boxing films. I had a brief cameo in Ron Shelton's "Play it to the Bone," which is about a fictional boxing match between two journeymen fighters. There's even a scene where one of the managers says, "Get Ratner on the phone!" I get a kick out of that because I know what it's like on the other end of those calls.

The other experience was even more surreal. On the Friday before officiating a game at Notre Dame, my crew had just left the bookstore on campus when I received a call. When I answered, a woman's voice came on, "Please hold for Mr. Stallone." Naturally I thought it wasn't real and was about to hang up when the unmistakable voice of Rocky himself came on the line. The whole crew was watching me and heard me say. "Hello, Mr. Stallone. How are you doing?" Of course, they thought I was pulling their leg until I put him on speaker phone. Then all of their eyes popped out. Stallone wanted to talk about the upcoming "Rocky" sequel, to be called "Rocky Balboa," which would be filmed at Mandalay Bay in Las Vegas. He asked me questions about the boxing commission and the weigh-in, reiterating that he wanted it to be authentic. Then he told me, "And of course, we want you to weigh the fighters." It was an amazing moment but strange. Here I was, as the Executive Director of the Nevada State Athletic Commission, and the world's most famous fictional fighter was asking me to do my job on camera for a fictional fight. Of course, I said yes.

A few months later I was standing in front of the scale weighing Rocky (Stallone) and Mason "The Line" Dixon (played by light heavyweight Antonio Tarver). As was my custom, and as Chuck Minker did it, I weighed the fighters with my back to the camera and then said my two lines: "Rocky Balboa, 217" and "Mason 'The Line' Dixon, 221." Right after that first take, Stallone—who directed the movie—jumped in. The idea of an actor keeping his back to the camera was anathema. "No, no, no" he said. "Marc, you gotta *face* the camera when you say that." So I did what he asked. Just that one time. I think Chuck would've understood; he would've gotten a huge kick out of the whole thing. I was in the fight scenes, as well, and the shooting was fascinating but really strange. I was watching a fictionalized version of something I've seen hundreds of times, among the extras and cardboard cutouts in the stands. The fight is tightly choreographed, and the actors don't actually hit each other; the gloves are a little bit longer, so it looks more authentic on screen. I've always loved boxing because of the element of the unexpected, but these fight scenes need to be planned down to the inch. It's strange watching the same thing happen over and over again. Sometimes it took a whole day to shoot one round. Of course, I don't remember the sitting around as much as I recall how incredible it all was, how it's something I can share with my grandkids.

With Sylvester Stallone and Antonio Tarver on the set of Rocky Balboa.

There's a performance aspect to all fighters. Very few of them, and none of the big names, can just go about their business in the ring and not develop an outsized persona, an exaggerated version of who they are. That's just part of being a big-time boxer. But it's an act—for most of them. Tyson himself said he was "the greatest actor who ever entered the ring." "Mike Tyson" was just a role that he played. As a person, Tyson was a bit of mystery. He always polite to me face-to-face, even when we were in the midst of reprimanding or punishing him. To this day he comes to the UFC office and is always kind and respectful.

The main issue with Mike was when the persona bled into the man. That's when the trouble arose. Around the time he entered retirement, he matured into a gentler person. His progression reminded me of George Foreman's, who also became a beloved figure after being viewed as nasty during his career. In retirement, Foreman became an affable character, TV celebrity and product pitchman. The longer you're away from the sport, often the better you look.

I spent a lot of time with fighters in our office and away from the spectacle, as I do now for UFC. Most of them are total gentlemen and women. Sometimes on fight night, with everyone screaming and their entourages around them hyping them up, they just aren't approachable in the same way. "When you have millions of dollars, you have millions of friends," heavyweight champ Floyd Patterson had once said. But most fighters are regular guys who have an unnatural talent and an irregular job. They show off for press conferences, try to get a rise out of the opponent, want to get endorsements, and think they can sell more tickets by putting on a show. This is not specific to boxing, but there is a long tradition in the sport of trying to get a rise out of people: press, opponents, fans. It's part of the show, and the fans expect it.

Oscar De La Hoya was one of the really special ones. Nicknamed "Golden Boy" by his promoter Bob Arum, he had both the style and substance. De La Hoya was a hard puncher, a gritty fighter, but he also had this mediagenic side. He knew how to present himself with "a clean-cut, corporate-friendly image."[28] Oscar was a congenial guy, funny in private. One time at a weigh-in, he pulled off his three sweatshirts and stepped on the scale. He was slightly over—which was unlike him—and I made a worried face. Oscar then started laughing and stripped off his heavy trunks, which I hadn't noticed. He got back on the scale and made weight.

The weigh-ins and press conferences were usually uneventful, mostly just staged events to bring attention to the fight. For heavyweights, they don't even have a weight to make, as there is no limit. It's really just theater, an opportunity for some pre-show hype. Sometimes this spilled over into antics, which caused a huge headache for me. When a scuffle broke out at a weigh-in or press conference, it brought some publicity to the fight and the sport, but it was usually a nightmare on my end. I was like the guy walking behind the elephant shoveling up the mess. The press loved it, and the fans got a kick out of it, but they didn't see what I saw: canceled fights, suspensions, fines, lost revenue, disappointed fans, and hearings—nothing that benefits the fighters or boxing as a whole.

I remember at the weigh-in for a highly anticipated fight between Jose Luis Castillo and Diego Corrales, Castillo stepped on the scale and was three pounds over. After a brief break—fighters have a window during which they can be weighed multiple times—he came back on. During the second try, one of Castillo's cornerman tried to put his foot under the scale to lift it. It was such a cheap and easily spotted trick, it was an insult to me and to the sport. I did this for a living, so of course I noticed it. I was ticked off. We fined him and banned him from the corner for the fight. Castillo ended up not making weight and was fined as well, though the fight still went on without a title at stake.

In August 2000, at the press conference before a fight between Fernando Vargas and Ross Thompson, Thompson ran across the stage to take a swing at Vargas, who struck back to defend himself. Then Gary Shaw, the promoter for Main Events, got hit standing in between them. Thompson had to be dragged away by security, and the commission fined him $10,000. We then had to redo the interrupted weigh in. Out of caution, the fighters came in to get weighed separately the next day.

Of course, Tyson's behavior during pre-fight events wasn't always the most gentlemanly or helpful. After a late hit against Norris that led to a no-contest in 1999[*], Tyson hadn't fought in Las Vegas for nearly three

---

[*] The late hit was deemed accidental, but this was a whole other headache.

years. In 2002, a Tyson-Lennox Lewis championship fight was scheduled for April that would've been a gigantic boon for MGM Grand, for the city, and the sport. Mike and Lennox knew each other going back to their amateur days, and there was a mutual dislike. On top of that, Tyson was clearly going through a volatile time, which wasn't news to us.

The press conference was held at the Hudson Theater in New York City in January. When HBO and Main Events called me beforehand, I reminded both of them, "Keep the fighters apart. You have the votes to fight here. We don't want to blow it. Whatever you do, don't pose them."

Twenty minutes later, that's exactly what they did.

At the press conference, each fighter was announced and came out to stand on a podium. After Lewis' announcement, Tyson walked over and reached for Lewis. When one of Lewis' guys got in his way, it sparked pandemonium, just an all-out melee. Tyson was enraged, and when the two fighters were rolling on the floor, Tyson bit Lewis' leg. After the fight broke up, Tyson was on TV saying vile things to a woman in the crowd and to one of the shocked reporters. After that, Tyson left us no choice. There was no way the state of Nevada was going to license him. The city and state lost millions, the MGM Grand lost a fortune, and the promoters had to shop the fight around. Most places honored our suspension but it eventually happened in Memphis in a few months later.

In retirement, Tyson has mellowed considerably. He seems happy with the world, and one could almost call him lovable now, which would've been the last word people would've used during his heyday. Now, when he walks into the arena, people just go nuts. He was doing a one-man show at the MGM Grand about his life which was quite good and well received. It's like there has been a mass forgiveness, at least for his boxing antics.[*] It reminds me a bit about what happened to Ali after he retired. Bygones become bygones. In our UFC office, we have conference rooms named after both Muhammad Ali and Mike Tyson[**],

---

[*] I'm not referring to his legal problems.
[**] There's also a statue in the lobby of UFC Headquarters of the immortal Joe Louis.

which says a lot about how his status has changed. Boxing history has treated him kindly.

Tyson and me in Atlantic City.

Coin flip before Holyfield-Lewis II, November 1999, as Don King looks on. Since both fighters were champions, I flipped a coin to determine who would enter the ring first and be announced last.

■ ■ ■

Lennox was a well-liked British fighter with a long reach, distinguished accent and congenial manner. He carried himself in a more classic gentleman style, but once inside the ring, he was a real fighter who could knockout opponents with either hand. He fought in Nevada eight times, in Lake Tahoe and at different hotels in Las Vegas. I remember he once brought his mother Violet, with whom he was very close, to Mandalay Bay to cook for him before his rematch against Hasim Rahman, who he knocked out.

Lewis was also part of two of the strangest fights in boxing history. Once he was matched against Henry Akinwande, who just refused to fight. Through five rounds he kept grabbing Lennox and not letting go. Eventually, referee Mills Lane had to disqualify him for excessive holding. In a fight that same year at the Las Vegas Hilton, Lennox fought Oliver McCall, who he dominated for the first three rounds. At the end of the third round, Oliver wouldn't go back to his corner. Then he started crying. Over the next couple of rounds, he completely lost focus and stopped even attempting to fight, so Mills had to give the TKO to Lennox. As fate would have it, Mills Lane was the referee for the "Fan Man" fight, the "Bite Fight," the Henry Akinwande fight, and Oliver McCall fight. It's what I call the "Grand Slam of Bizarreness."

Though Lewis was a great champion, he didn't have the impact of Tyson. The next fighter who really garnered that kind of mass attention was welterweight Floyd Mayweather Jr. Floyd had a rough upbringing in Michigan, with a father who was a felon and drug trafficker. "When I was little, I lived seven deep in a one-bedroom apartment," he once said. "Seeing somebody shot, seeing a gun… that is normal for me."[29] He had a lot of strikes against him, but he impressively rose above his circumstances to become a legend.

Floyd's father and two uncles Jeff and Roger (who became his trainer) were fighters, too. From a young age, Floyd Jr. poured himself entirely into the craft of boxing and became a prodigy. He is not just a phenomenal athlete and fighter, but he's a student of the game. He knows all about other fighters' strengths and weaknesses and their histories. He had most of his fights here in Las Vegas, and I've probably seen him fight 25 times, including his pro debut. We have a friendly relationship. He always comes over to talk to me, and I see him at UNLV games and at other fights. In the ring, Floyd was something special, a tremendous talent. Very seldom was he ever hit flush; he just instinctively knew how to move his body and his head, how to "roll with the punches," as they say. It's like nothing ever landed on the guy. Few opponents ever hit him square or hurt him at all. Even when Floyd did get hit, he had a strong enough chin to take it. I remember Shane Mosley once hit him and buckled him a bit early in a fight. Then Floyd beat him up pretty good, winning every round after that. It was like Floyd punished him for getting a good shot on him.

Another aspect of Floyd's success was that he is a brilliant marketer. He went to WrestleMania and on "Dancing with The Stars", garnering new fans along the way. After starting out as "Pretty Boy," he switched his nickname to "Money." He became a heel, quoted saying outrageous things about rich he was and how he spent his money, posting pictures of himself hitting the jackpot for $100,000, flashing cash and cars and jewelry. He understood that 21st Century sports stardom required self-promotion. In the old days, someone like Don King could talk for you. These days, fans expect to hear from you directly and regularly. Floyd was masterful at it, understanding how to use social media, capitalizing on Instagram and Twitter followings to build his showman persona.

Floyd was undefeated, a staggering 49-0, when he retired. It's as impressive a feat as any athlete has achieved in sports. (He is now 50-0 since the McGregor fight). As impressive as that record is, it doesn't tell the whole story of his dominance. In my opinion, he has only had one real close fight: the first match against Jose Luis Castillo in April 2002 at MGM Grand for the WBC Lightweight Title. Floyd was moving up to the lightweight division that night, where Castillo held the title. Although Floyd was a 4-to-1 favorite, Castillo really made it close. It's the only time I remember seeing Floyd really battling. He came out aggressive and landed a lot of good shots in those first four rounds, but then there was a switch. Floyd was much better when they were in the middle of the ring, so Castillo backed Floyd into the ropes to get clearer shots on him. At the end of the fight, the HBO team had Castillo by five points, so the TV crowd likely saw it that way, too. The judges ruled unanimously in Floyd's favor (by four and five points), a deficit that even Mayweather's promoter Bob Arum called "overzealous." It was a controversial decision, to say the least. The crowd was pro-Castillo, and they were fighting on the weekend of Mexican Independence Day. When the decision was announced, a sea of boos rumbled across the arena. It was like a wave that kept rising and falling. That was another one of those Mondays when the phone rang all day, and I had to field complaints from those who thought Castillo was robbed. Of course, I took as many calls as I could.

Mayweather was such a large presence during my final years with the commission, and the last major fight I oversaw was one of his—the infamous contest against Zab Judah. It was in April 2006 at the Thomas & Mack Center in Las Vegas, about a month before I left. Zab was one of Don King's fighters. He was as quick as Floyd, which is saying something. But he had a history of letting his emotions get in the way of his fighting. In his previous fight, against Kostya Tszyu, one of Kostya's punches knocked him down. After Zab got back up, he had trouble standing. His legs flailed like two noodles for a moment. He had an involuntary spastic response and fell back down. That was all the referee, Jay Nady, needed to see. He stopped the fight immediately, which was absolutely the right decision. But Zab's reaction went well over the line. He went over to Jay and put his glove on Jay's chin. He had to be pulled away, and then he threw a stool in the ring. Zab completely lost his temper that night, and the commission had to come down on him.

The first four rounds of the fight against Mayweather were pretty even, with Zab staying right with him, getting solid hits in pretty consistently. Then Floyd, who is a very smart fighter, made some adjustments and took control. With 10 seconds left in the tenth round,

Zab hit Floyd really low, causing Floyd to bend over in pain. Then Zab hit him with a quick shot behind the head before the referee sent him to the neutral corner. Floyd's uncle and trainer Roger jumped through the ropes to go after Zab. Then Zab's father, Yoel, jumped through the ropes and Leonard Ellerbe, Mayweather's advisor, got into it with Yoel Judah. There was a gigantic fracas, with cops, security and cornermen flooding into the ring. It was mayhem.

What I remember more than anything was Floyd going to a neutral corner, putting his hand on the ropes and watching it all unfold from a distance, refusing to get involved. He was smart enough to know that no good would come of it. I was up on the apron, holding onto the ropes like they were a bucking bronco. I was not sure where to look because the fight was moving from one side of the ring to the other, and bodies were getting tossed from the circle.

Once it calmed down, I climbed into the ring and walked over to Richard Steele, the referee. I wanted to hear his thoughts about how to handle the situation. The commission was later criticized for not disqualifying Floyd after Roger jumped into the ring, but that didn't make sense, nor was it fair. Floyd was the recipient of the fouls that triggered the scuffle, and he did nothing wrong. Eventually we were able to clear the ring and get back to the scheduled fight, but it took some time. Later, we watched all the footage, from HBO's overview cameras and from the sides to figure out the penalties. The commission fined and suspended Roger Mayweather, Zab Judah, and his father Yoel for a year Judah for a year and Leonard Ellerbe for four months. That fight was my last major controversy. I didn't know at the time that a whole new chapter was about to be written in combat sports, and I would be invited to play a part of it.

CHAPTER TEN

■ ■ ■

Joining the Fight

"You get it, Marc. You understand what we're trying to do." I was sitting across from Lorenzo Fertitta at a cafe inside Palace Station, a casino he owned and ran with his brother, Frank. Lorenzo is handsome with light blue eyes, closely cropped hair and goatee. At the time he was in his mid-30s, an accomplished guy who was approachable and friendly. Plenty of people dropped by to shake his hand during our meal, and he smoothly managed all of them.

I always had liked Lorenzo, and our rapport was helped by the fact that I knew him back when he was one of the commissioners at the Nevada State Athletic Commission in the 1990s. Actually, I knew him even further back—when he was a standout defensive back for Bishop Gorman High School, and I was a referee. Whenever we got together, we'd reminisce. He'd remind me how often I threw penalty flags on him, which might've been true.*

In 2001, the Fertitta brothers bought the struggling Ultimate Fighting Championship for $2 million** and brought in their old

---

* Danny Tarkanian's mom at UNLV would get on me for my quick whistle as well.
** As of 2020, UFC is valued at over $4 billion.

friend Dana White to run it. UFC was a mixed martial arts (MMA) league that had been around since 1993 as more of a sideshow, but the Fertitta brothers and Dana were working to reboot it as a mainstream sport. Lorenzo had said he and his brother were really just buying some old tapes and the letters U-F-C. They and Dana saw what it could be. I had dealings with all three of them around 2001 when Nevada first licensed the sport in our state. I assumed the breakfast meeting had something to do with a regulatory matter, but I was way off.

We talked about a few things, and then he put down his fork, like punctuation. "So, Marc, I've been talking to Dana and Frank. We're thinking we might have some ideas for you." He was being purposely vague, and I wasn't sure I understood what he meant.

Seeing no reason to pretend, I told him. "Ideas for what exactly?" I asked.

He rephrased: "Have you ever thought about leaving the commission?"

The words were a slight shock, and I put down my tea. It took me a moment to absorb the question. "Well," I said, "that sure is an interesting idea, but I really haven't. I honestly feel like I have the best regulatory job in the world." I was telling the truth. I had never thought of leaving. Las Vegas had the best fights, and I loved my job: doing the weigh-ins, the bright lights, the ringside seats, the excitement of fight night and my place in it.

That's when Lorenzo launched into how I understood what UFC was trying to do, that I "got it," that my relationship with all the state commissions would be an asset. It was flattering that they had discussed bringing me in, but I honestly didn't think much of it at the time. There was nothing concrete, but it was clear he was feeling me out. A little intrigued, but mostly to be polite, I told him I'd be happy to talk some more at a later date.

Running the Nevada State Athletic Commission had been a dream job for nearly 15 years, and I just imagined I'd do it forever. But the commission was changing. Dr. Nave had moved on, Dr. Ghanem had passed away, and I had turned 60 the previous year. Maybe I was ripe for a new opportunity. At home, I mentioned the Lorenzo meeting to my wife, Jody, more as a strange thing than a real possibility. Then I put it in the back of my mind.

About a month later, sometime around Thanksgiving, Lorenzo's assistant called me to schedule another breakfast meeting at Palace Station. This one had a completely different tenor because it had one major difference: Dana White. White was a former boxer, boxercise coach and UFC fighter manager who possessed unbridled enthusiasm that is just infectious. He did not soft pedal with me, going in for the hard sell before our breakfast even arrived.

"Listen, Marc," Dana launched in, his deep and raspy voice cutting through the restaurant's noise. "We've talked about this a lot, and our vision for UFC is to make it the next NFL." Dana is built like a fighter, and his broad shoulders took up most of the booth. "I'm being straight with you: You are absolutely part of that plan, our top choice for this job. You understand the sport, you know the commissions, and you can help us grow in a regulatory sense. We're only in around 20 states at the moment and we see ourselves getting much bigger." As he got into the flow of his pitch, his whole frame leaned in and his intensity grew. "You have the experience, the relationships, and the integrity to make UFC the next big thing. We need you. Are you interested?"

I was taken aback, not expecting something so direct. Also, I was thrown because I really clicked with Dana's pitch: *Come help build the future.* When it was put that way, it sounded exciting. UFC had come a long way, even in just the four years since Lorenzo and Frank had bought it. (Dana himself had said the original UFC was "absolutely nuts"). But the sport still had a way to go before it could reach the mainstream: to be as popular as boxing, yes, but also as popular as leagues like NASCAR and NFL. Lorenzo and Dana pitched me as central to that growth and maturation process. They were also interested in what I represented. Boxing was a combat sport, but it was accepted as part of America—a piece of the country's history and heritage. So, bringing in an old boxing hand, an established "rules guy" no less, someone who had been working in boxing since the days of Hagler and Leonard, brought legitimacy to MMA by association.

I knew not to underestimate them. They had already rescued the sport from its seemingly inevitable demise and reversed it from near oblivion. By 2005, at the time of my meeting with Dana, UFC was on its way, shifting from spectacle to sport. While some in boxing may have turned up their noses, I smelled the future.

My history with UFC began almost 10 years before that first meeting with Lorenzo. In 1996, I was invited to appear on "Larry King Live," along with Senator John McCain, to discuss how UFC was dangerous and why perhaps it should be banned. Arguing for UFC that night was fighter Ken Shamrock and UFC owner and co-founder Bob Meyerowitz. The sport began in the early '90s as the brainchild of jiu-jitsu master Rorion Gracie and ad executive Art Davie, who both thought of the idea of staging a tournament to determine which type of martial arts was the "ultimate." At the time, the sport was leaning heavily into controversy ("No-holds-barred combat," and "Two men enter and one leaves.") and was intentionally dangerous. When it first began, there were no weight classes, no gloves, and only three rules: no eye gouging, no biting and no groin striking. The referee wasn't even allowed to stop the fight. Fortunately, they came to their senses and changed that rule by the third event.[30] But it was still too dangerous, in my opinion, and I said so publicly. This was not a controversial view at the time. Because of Nevada's place at the center of the boxing world, our impression of MMA held a lot of weight. Senator McCain was chairman of the commerce committee, which oversaw pro sports, and was a former Navy boxer. He led the charge against UFC, famously labeling it "human cockfighting" and had written letters to governors recommending they ban it in their states. At the time, I agreed 100 percent.

Sports, by definition, means rules. A fight without rules is not a sport; it's just a fight. UFC was too violent, too hazardous, and not something we were interested in sanctioning or hosting in Nevada.

"We just can't have a sport here that advertises no rules," I said outright on the air. The pitch for UFC went against my very nature as a regulator. My purpose in combat sports—from my days as an inspector to Executive Director of the athletic commission—was to give a frame and foundation to the fight. Getting rid of rules was getting rid of sport itself.

Senator McCain's campaign was effective, and in the late 1990s, UFC was in and out of court and nearly bankrupt. Fights were being moved at the last minute, major markets wouldn't sanction it, and the cable companies wouldn't show it. Eventually it ran so low on money that it was essentially on life support. When the Fertitta brothers bought UFC for only $2 million, it was regulated in only one state: New Jersey. The previous owners had been going to states without athletic commissions specifically to avoid regulation. But the Fertitta brothers and Dana had a brilliant plan: they were going to run toward regulation. Lorenzo came from the same background as me. He understood how to save the sport. Very few businesses ever ask to be regulated, but it was a genius move on their part. It saved UFC, allowed it to grow, and eventually turned it into a juggernaut.

In 2000, the Fertitta brothers began working with the New Jersey Athletic Commission under the auspices of Commissioner Larry Hazzard and Deputy Attorney General Nick Lembo to write a set of rules so the sport could be regulated in other states. I was invited to contribute. The goal was to bring standards and safety to the fights without draining the sport of what appealed to its fans. The first step for me was getting an education. They sent me a box of DVDs, and I got to work learning the ins and outs of MMA. I had a loose knowledge of kickboxing, which we regulated in Nevada, but this was something totally new. As I watched, I had to keep hitting the pause button and rewinding, trying to make sense of what I saw. What first threw me was that when someone knocked down his opponent, he could then keep hitting him while he was on the ground. This was not just against the rules in boxing; it was against the very *point* of boxing! Where a boxing match ends, MMA fights were just getting started.

Once I absorbed that idea, it opened up the uniqueness of MMA fights, the strategy, and the versatility of the fighters. My initial thoughts was that the guy on top was automatically winning, but I came to learn that wasn't always true. Sometimes the fighter who was brought to the ground *wanted* to be brought to the ground; he may have even been the one who made it happen. A fighter who was up against a strong striker *wanted* to go to the ground where grappling would determine the outcome. From there, he angled to take control of the fight, even from the bottom position.* The top fighter sometimes had trouble getting the same leverage on the ground that he had standing up; he couldn't get his whole body behind those punches. It was counterintuitive to my experience and it was complex, a type of chess. Some of these fighters were planning two or three moves ahead, trying to create a position where they could gain advantage.

In that way it wasn't too different from boxing, where there had to be strategy. This is why good corners come into play for both sports. A strong corner will notice things and make adjustments in the strategy.

The way fights ended also stood out to me. An MMA fight didn't conclude with a 10-count. Getting knocked down changed the fight but didn't end it, unless the fighter was unable to defend himself. Once that happened, it was over. So, I had to watch and study the referees to see what constituted that particular standard—when they stepped in and when they let the fight continue. I also saw that most MMA fighters had a wider stance than boxers, protecting themselves from being easily kicked out of it. In addition, they were punching from further away. If being too close in boxing could tie you up, getting too close in MMA could take you down. Strikers had something akin to a boxing stance, while wrestlers and ground-game fighters kept their feet more parallel. While kickboxers had foot padding, MMA fighters

---

* I use "he" here—and throughout—for clarity but obviously men and women both compete in combat sports.

were barefoot and their leg and foot dexterity was astounding. Some used their feet to jab the opponent, targeting exact spots on upper legs, thighs, and shins. I also had to wrap my mind around the set-up: a giant eight-sided, fenced-in structure called the Octagon, instead of a square ring with ropes. I had to understand how the fence affected the fight and even the presentation of the fight, what the entrances entailed, where the cornermen sat since there were no corners, where the referees and judges sat, and how the spectators viewed it. After 15 years in boxing, this required a mind shift.

I learned about legal and illegal hits, a list which we would add to during our meeting. There were illegal hits in boxing, too, but when an MMA fight went to the ground it was much harder to spot them. MMA did not allow eye pokes, fish hooks,* kicking or kneeing a downed opponent in the head, headbutting, or grabbing the fence or an opponent's shorts. Elbows are legal in MMA, though now they have to come in on an angle. They can't be straight on, like 12-to-6 on a clock.

The rules meeting with Commissioner Hazzard and Deputy Attorney General Lembo of the New Jersey Athletic Commission took place in Newark in April 2001. I "attended" on the phone for around four hours. In person for UFC were Lorenzo, Dana, Kirk Hendrick and matchmaker Joe Silva, along with various other officials and MMA stakeholders. Others were helpful in the MMA rules writing process, including referee John McCarthy and Jeff Blatnick, a 1984 Olympic gold medalist in Greco-Roman wrestling. By the end of the meeting, we had come up with the Unified Rules of MMA, which included more than 30 actions fighters couldn't do. New Jersey adopted the rules right away, and not long after, Nevada was able to approve and sanction the sport.

The first MMA fight I ever saw live was also the first event in Nevada and the first one we regulated: UFC 33. It took place in

---

* This is what is sounds like—putting a finger into an opponent's mouth and pulling.

late September 2001 at Mandalay Bay. We weren't sure what kind of crowd we'd have in the weeks after 9/11. People weren't flying or vacationing, and the country was in a somber mood. It was one the first major sporting events since the terrorist attacks, and we had no idea what to expect. Since I'd never seen a UFC fight in person before, I *really* didn't know what to expect.

I got there a couple hours early, and there already was a crowd inside Mandalay Bay, snaking around the venue waiting to get in. In all my years of boxing, I had never seen that. Once inside, even before the first fight, the crowd had this energy, a sense of defiance about them that cut against all the apprehension and fear in the air at the time in our country. It was powerful to be standing among it. That night was electric, something different and undeniable. The crowd had more of a pep-rally-meets-rock-concert feel. Back then, the UFC audience was mostly young males, but in the intervening years, that has changed. The audience has expanded into all ages, genders, and backgrounds.

There were three title fights on the card that night–a lineup that also included one of the rising stars of that era, Chuck Liddell, and future star Matt Serra. The main event was a contest between one of UFC's first big names, Tito Ortiz, and Vladimir "The Janitor" Matyushenko from Belarus. Another element that was new for me was that the early fighters were not "undercards" in the classic sense. Those 5 p.m. fights could be just as exciting as the main event. And the crowd knew it.

Taking it all in live was so much different than it was from my living room: the energy from the crowd, the spectacle of each fighter's entrance, the blasting music and light show and thudding of bodies hitting the canvas. As a one-time inspector, I kept my eye on the corners and the referees, trying to see what they were seeing. Since wrestling is part of the fight, the inspectors needed to check for excessive Vaseline on the fighter, which would make him too slippery to grab. The gloves were four to six ounces, much smaller than boxing gloves, so it was harder to hide anything in them, though there was still a wrapping protocol.

In those days, there was a big ramp that came right down to the Octagon for fighters to enter. They soon realized the ramp was going through some of the most expensive seats and moved it to the sides. There were other differences back in 2001, but there were still three judges, a referee, and the scoring was the same. It was called a "10-Point Must System", which we devised as part of the Unified Rules. The winner of the round must get 10 points, and the loser gets 9 or fewer. Fouls can take points away.

MMA fights ended differently, too. Unlike boxing, it was considered honorable to give up, to "tap out." In boxing, if you quit on the stool, it became infamous, like Roberto Duran's "no mas" or Liston not coming out in the seventh round against Ali. In MMA, if you got into a hold you couldn't get out of, tapping out was like doffing your hat. It was a different culture of fighting. *You beat me, I accept it.* It was almost noble, and I appreciated that element of it.

Just about every fight that night went the distance or went to decision, so it ran long. The Pay-Per-View feed cut off during the main event, so if you were watching at home, you missed it. Viewers were angry and demanded refunds. It was an important lesson for UFC, and it never once happened again.* Dana was open about the fact that UFC 33 was underwhelming, mostly because of all the decisions, but as I had nothing to compare it to, I found it memorable. Nevertheless, I had no concept in my mind that this was where my future would lead. At the time, the thought had never occurred to me.

A little over four years after I watched my first live UFC event, I was offered a chance to be a part of it. During Christmas break, I talked it over with a few mentors and with my wife Jody. She was surprised that I was even considering leaving—she too thought I'd be with the commission for life. But she also knew that the idea of something

---

* On top of everything else that night, right after the fights ended, I had to hustle to catch a midnight flight to Phoenix and then San Diego so I could officiate a college football game the next day.

new was getting my juices flowing. She supported whatever decision I came to, but gave me one piece of advice. "At least get a contract."

In February, there was a third meeting, this time with just Lorenzo again and a hard offer. I didn't ask what my title would be, but it was clear that I'd be an executive in charge of regulation. There was some discussion of my duties, how I'd have to fly to New York once in a while and maybe a few other American cities. (There was no talk of traveling the world, which is what ended up happening.) The fact that regulators around the country knew me would help UFC's case. *If Ratner is vouching for the legitimacy of this sport, maybe we should reconsider or take another look…*

We had a big boxing match coming up that February, so I dragged my feet a little, waiting to put that behind me. In March, the media got wind that I was considering joining UFC. That triggered a call from Lorenzo, who cut right to the chase. "Ok, look," he said. "It's out there. Are you gonna come or not?" It was a moment of truth. I told him I was in. I had one major fight on Cinco de Mayo weekend with Oscar de La Hoya and Ricardo Margarito at the MGM Grand, and after that, I'd be there.

Once the news started to break, I called Dr. Nave and Bob Arum and, of course, the staff. Colleen was very unhappy; she heard about it before I told her. It was emotional. I worked with them for 14 years, but once the shock wore off, she was fine. No one thought I'd ever leave. A five man-commission chose the successor. I met with my successor, Keith Kizer, to let him know I was leaving. He was the deputy attorney general for gaming, and the athletic commission was under his purview. "I want you to think about it, if you're interested," I said. "It would be a seamless transition."

Everyone held a nice farewell party for me, hosted by ring announcer Jake Gutierrez. They presented a tribute video produced by Showtime and a career-spanning boxing highlight video. People from all over went to the podium and said some words: people from the governor's office, from the state, from the commission, from the IRS and from businesses.

Boxing officials presented me with a gift and plaque they had made with my lacquered shoes on them, and Dr. Nave was there, whose presence I appreciated. It is not in my nature to be comfortable with the spotlight, but I was touched by the graciousness of the ceremony and the kindness of all my colleagues made me feel as though I had made a lasting impact, which is the most anyone can ask for in his work.

Most people were supportive, though some in the boxing world gave me a hard time and told me UFC was never going to last. They didn't see it as a legitimate competitor, just a scrappy upstart, a stunt-type of thing. No one thought it had a chance to become like boxing. "It'll never get traction," they said, thinking it was crazy for me to leave the center of the boxing world for something they didn't understand. "What are you doing going into MMA? You're going to regret it someday, and you're going to want to come back." They didn't see what I saw, which came from what Dana saw: an extension of combat sports, with the potential to appeal to youth and the new generation in ways that boxing didn't. Dana knew there was a public relations element to hiring me, that it would change the perception in the sports and fight community. Putting my face on regulation was one way of announcing he was serious about taking UFC into the mainstream.

I talked to Mr. Arum about it before the news was out. "If it's better for you…" he said, "…better for your family, go for it." Mr. A is an old-school guy, and he was totally supportive. I'm sure when he left law to join boxing, he got pushback, so he understood where I was coming from. To this day, I still run into Mr. A at temple on high holidays, and he's always gracious.

I admit that Dana was a big part of my decision. I didn't know him well, but I could tell he was like a comet that you wanted to catch a ride on. I was right: there's not a single leader of any sport who can go toe-to-toe with him in terms of love and passion for their sport. Nothing is half-measure with him, and if he thinks something is worth doing, he goes all-in. He's both a leader and a fan, and that combination got me excited. When some commissioners are at a draft or press conference, they have a stilted way about them. Not Dana. He is of the sport in an organic way, and the fans and fighters love that about him.

Of course, the largest reason I took the job was the opportunity to grow a sport—which is very rare. Everyone wants some kind of legacy, and very few people get a chance to be on the ground floor of a sport. Even though it had been around for 13 years by that point, that all felt like prologue. In 2006, it was building momentum out of the world of niche sports into something bigger, something that was taking sports fans by storm, something that felt of the 21st Century. Looking back almost 15 years later, it's so clear to me I made the right choice. Aside from marrying my wife and having my children, it was the best decision I've ever made.

CHAPTER ELEVEN

■ ■ ■

The Quest for 50

But it was far from glamorous. Building the future never is. My official UFC title was Vice President of Regulatory and Government Affairs. It was combat sports, and I'd be dealing with many of the people I'd worked with at the Nevada State Athletic Commission. But there were discrete differences about my new job. For one, there were fewer people working for UFC back in 2006, and they skewed younger. When I first came over, I wore a buttoned-down, collared shirt and slacks, my typical work uniform for going on 25 years, going back to my days in advertising. I noticed Dana White wandering around in a t-shirt and jeans, and since he was in charge, others followed his lead, dressing informally. That was my first cue. "Hey, Marc," one of the younger guys in the office told me after a meeting. "You know you don't have to you wear a shirt and tie or anything like that. Just make yourself comfortable."

I was no longer a state employee, so the atmosphere was different around the office, more casual. There was a young and fun vibe that was contagious. We weren't a bureaucracy working with taxpayer dollars; we were more like explorers on a new frontier. That element brought some extra excitement. We weren't keeping something running like a well-tuned machine, which the commission was doing. We were setting up the machine, breaking new ground.

First those first few months, I was getting situated and immersing myself in the process. When I arrived, we had fights going on and scheduled, so I hit the ground running. I began working on assignments for referees and judges in Nevada and in other states, especially on the east coast in New Jersey and Pennsylvania. I'd advise their commissions on officials from our end of the country, who I knew well.

But the big task for me, for all of us, was getting MMA approved and regulated around the country. The Fertitta brothers and Dana wanted the sport legalized in all 50 states; they knew UFC's future depended on it. So, I got to work. At the time, there were around 20 states that allowed MMA, and we were heading into an uphill battle getting the sport legalized everywhere in the U.S. The marketing campaign that helped give UFC publicity in the 1990s—the death-match type language—was our biggest hurdle. For years after the passage of the Unified Rules of MMA in 2001, plenty of government officials, and even media members, still had a preconceived notion of what UFC was.

I began by first getting a lay of the land: an understanding of where the sport wasn't approved, what obstacles might be in our way, of who I needed to talk to, and where I needed to go. Plenty of people at UFC were integral to the process, like Chief Operating Officer Lawrence Epstein, Kirk Hendrick, Dana and Lorenzo, but my partner in the quest for 50 states was Mike Mersch, a former deputy attorney general who I knew from time on the commission. Mike was a lawyer, six feet tall, and good looking—the kind of guy who walks in a room and women turn their heads. We traveled together from state to state, hopscotching across the nation to different capitals, living in hotels, sleeping on planes, and getting to know each other pretty well during what turned out to be a 10-year battle.* Having a

---

* Mike went on to private practice and now works with several fighters, including Conor McGregor.

lawyer alongside me was essential because there were legal hurdles in approving MMA, which also meant other lawyers had to be consulted and convinced. Mike was integral to the legislative planning for each state, and we made a good team.

In states with athletic commissions, sometimes we just had to work with them to add MMA regulations to their pre-existing framework. Usually, it was not that easy. We started with places like Michigan, Illinois, and New York—states with big cities. New York was a huge obstacle, having banned MMA in 1997 at the height of the sport's bad press. Our biggest obstacles were states (like New York) that had statutes in the law that only applied to boxing or specifically banned MMA. We had to go to state capitol offices and deal with the legislative bodies, sometimes for years. You can't just walk into a state senator or assembly person's office with your request. We first had to hire lobbyists, who make the whole machine work. They are the mediators that give you the opportunity to petition or meet face-to-face with the government, to get you five or 15 or 30 minutes to present your issue. Lobbyists know who's who, where the levers of persuasion are, which paths are least resistant, and how to get your case heard. Most importantly, they had pre-existing relationships with lawmakers and an understanding of the process, so they devised the game plan. We would've gotten nowhere without them.

In the state houses, the response we got depended on the history of the sport—if any—in that state, the culture there around other combat sports like boxing, and often, the age of the people we were dealing with. If it was with older or more conservative folks who didn't know much about MMA, we had a tougher sell. In places like Virginia, Wisconsin, and New Hampshire, we were dealing with legislators who hadn't seen any fights and knew little about it. All they knew was how violent it was. Some female legislators were openly aghast at the prospect of the sport in their state. Mike and I were entering into these meetings at a considerable disadvantage; they knew one thing about our product, and it was that they didn't want anything to do with it.

That put the onus on us to educate them, show the art and skill involved in MMA, going over the health and safety regulations in place, and explain the evolution of UFC. There were elected officials, along with their staff, who thought the sport was still "no holds barred," and I would use my own history to argue our case. "Wait. MMA?" they'd say, a familiar flicker in their eyes, "Isn't that like human cockfighting? Like John McCain called it?"

"Well, back then, it kind of was," I'd say. "I was actually on 'Larry King' with Senator McCain to speak out against it. We were against the sport because it had no rules." Then I'd explain the Unified Rules of MMA, the Fertitta brothers' and Dana's approach of moving toward regulation, and how we had approved it in Nevada after years of being against it. It had changed. "UFC today is not *that* UFC," I'd explain. "They may share a name, but that's about it."

I'd then talk about how it was spreading to other states (and countries), how boxing mainstays like Nevada and New Jersey had already approved it, how there were weight classes and officials and rules and athletic commissions overseeing it, just like anything else. On those trips, we worked to normalize their impression of MMA, which took some time and legwork. If the lawmakers were younger or had a younger staff, they knew a little bit more about UFC. This is a credit to Dana, who knew the public relations front was going to be a huge part of our battle. He had been laying the groundwork to publicize the sport over the years. Dana understood something elemental: if the public knew the fighters, had a relationship with them, *cared* about them, then they would become drawn to the matches.

The year before I arrived, in 2005, Dana and Lorenzo had the brilliant idea to do a reality show on Spike TV called "The Ultimate Fighter," which was a big hit. (This was back when reality TV was spreading but before it was everywhere.) The show was like our Trojan Horse, bringing MMA into people's living rooms. It helped get UFC positive attention, gave people a way to invest in the fighters, and brought new fans to the fights, either as live spectators or television viewers. In the next few years, the Fertitta brothers consolidated the sport by buying other promotions like WEC, WFA, and PRIDE in Japan, bringing all those fighters to the UFC roster. This expanded the pool of fighters, which raised the overall caliber, improved match-ups, expanded the locations of the fighters and their fan bases, and varied the styles of fighting.

Each year, Mike and I were working from a stronger negotiating position. We were able to pitch to states that they were going to miss the boat: *Don't you want to be part of this?*

We also dealt with athletic commissions who didn't really care about MMA and seemed averse to the extra work of having to learn and regulate a new sport. Their attitude was clearly, *We're not getting paid more, so why bother?* That happened in a few states, and most glaringly, in Canada, where we first met with the Ontario Commission in Toronto. They had a small staff and a manageable workload; if MMA was approved, it might be overwhelming for them. We spent time working with the commission on their regulations, which actually required the changing of a federal law. Then we hired our lobbyists and had to travel to the Canadian capital, Ottawa. I knew the commission's director from boxing, and he was straight with me: *You guys don't have a chance.* But we proved him wrong. In 2013, MMA became legal in Canada. But we didn't celebrate. There was so much more to do.

I kept a U.S. map in my office which marked all the states where MMA was legalized (in green) and illegal (in red). In 2007, we started flipping from red to green, like dominoes sweeping through the country. But New York still sat there as a glaring red "no." To help convince New York lawmakers, Dana and his people had been working the public relations angle for a while, making a big push in the media, bringing attention to the fights we held across the Hudson River at the Meadowlands and Prudential Center in New Jersey, dangling UFC's tax and business revenue.

Lawmakers always care about bringing money and tax revenue to their state, so we talked with legislators about the economic benefits of our live events. When the UFC came to town, the fighters and officials arrived almost a week early and would go to restaurants, rent cars and hotel rooms, see the sites, and engage with the city. It was like a mini convention. Between our staff, production team, the fighters, their camps, and their families, we would take more than 200 rooms in the host hotel. That translates into 500 to 600 room nights, which is substantial—a lot of money before you even sell a ticket, a concession, or a piece of merchandise. The fans arrived at the end of the week, some from far away, and they do the same: eat and drink and sleep and spend. If a UFC event was held in Cincinnati, Orlando, or Kansas City, for example, fans from outlying areas (and even from other states), knew that might be the closest a UFC event would ever come to them. They would flood in, not wanting to miss their chance.

There was a momentum angle to our work, as well. When one state legalized us, we'd talk to border states about how MMA had just been approved next door. In Oregon, we pitched how Washington, California, and Nevada already had it, and they were missing out. If economic revenue was coming in right over the border, legislators would be more likely to get on board. As the years passed, state after state flipped. But, still, we couldn't celebrate. One state remained stubbornly and conspicuously red—New York.

I felt like Captain Ahab in "Moby Dick" chasing that giant white whale that New York had become for UFC. It was the last place the sport had to exist if it was to be considered mainstream. Las Vegas and Atlantic City, even Los Angeles were important, but without New York City, we were not finished. In order to be anything in the sports world, you had to be able to hold events in Madison Square Garden, "The World's Most Famous Arena."

Approval in New York state took us almost eight years and around 30 trips to Albany—a city and a group of lawmakers with whom I became intimately familiar. Just like in the U.S. Congress, state legislatures are split into two houses: The Senate and the Assembly, which is like the House of Representatives. Every year for six years, we passed the Senate but couldn't even get a vote in the Assembly. The reason for that was one man: New York Assembly Speaker, Sheldon

Silver. There are 150 members of the Assembly, and we needed to have at least 76 of them to get a vote for MMA approval. The unwritten policy in the New York Assembly was not only did you need at least 76 votes, but none of them could come from the Republican side of the aisle. We always had close to the 76 votes, but we could never reach the magic number and had to come back to the next session and work on the Assembly members again. Depending on how you looked at it, it was politics at its best or at its worst.

The fighters themselves played a big role and came to Albany to help educate and lobby with us. During our campaign in New York, the list of fighters who supported our push was substantial: Matt Hughes, Chris Weidman, Jon Jones, Rashad Evans, Matt Serra, Uriah Hall, Ryan LaFlare, Liz Carmouche, and perhaps the sport's biggest name at the time, Ronda Rousey. They all understood what a big deal it was to get approved in New York. Rousey also appeared on "Late Night with Jimmy Fallon" to argue for our case, correctly pointing out that unregulated MMA, which was legal in New York, was far more dangerous than UFC. What brought a smile to my face was that some of the very same legislators voting against us were the first in line to have their picture taken with Ronda. That told me all I needed to know about which way the wind was blowing.

What was most frustrating about the entire experience was that the root of the problem had absolutely nothing to do with mixed martial arts. The Fertitta brothers also owned a company called Station Casinos in Las Vegas, and in Las Vegas, the Culinary Union is extremely powerful. The workers at Station Casinos were not unionized, so its sister union, the New York Hotel and Motel Trades Council (HTC), pressured union-dependent Democrat Shelly Silver to prevent MMA's legalization. What was happening in Vegas was not staying in Vegas. The objection had nothing to do with our sport or what was good for New York. It was a revenge plot hatched by a union across the country that was using a dishonest politician. (Ironically, having UFC events in New York would bring work and actually be a huge boon to the local unions. This fact made our case even stronger.) As speaker of the state assembly, Silver had the gavel, which meant he decided what bills did and did not come to the floor for a vote. As UFC Chief Operating Officer Lawrence Epstein said, Silver "was the guy who decided what happened or what didn't happen in the state of New York."

In 2011 we filed a lawsuit against the state, claiming its ban on MMA was unconstitutional. One of our arguments was that the ban didn't make sense. People were allowed to learn, practice, and compete in MMA in gyms and dojos all around the state, and everyone was allowed to watch it on TV. The ban really only prevented live events, not New Yorkers' exposure to the sport. We pushed the same argument to lawmakers that we made elsewhere: your citizens are watching and following UFC anyway. This way you at least get to share in the benefits. Also, the process was corrupt. *Whether you support the sport or not, at least let it go to a vote.*

One person was hamstringing the democratic process. It was wrong, even un-American, which I said in public. Silver took umbrage with me saying that, but I was right. Then in 2015, the chickens came home to roost.

Silver was indicted on federal corruption charges, ultimately sentenced to six and a half years in prison and a $1 million fine[*] and was expelled from the state assembly. With Silver gone, the tide swung almost instantly, which only proved how instrumental he had been in stonewalling us. Governor Andrew Cuomo openly pushed for legalization and said he would sign the bill if it got to his desk. In 2016, the new speaker gave us a vote and we won handily, 114 to 26. That night after the vote, we finally broke out the champagne and allowed ourselves to celebrate.

There were several people who played a big part in finally getting MMA legalized. We could not have gotten this done without Dana, Lorenzo, Lawrence Epstein, Kirk Hendrick, Mike Britt and Mike Mersch. The lobby firm of David Weinraub and Associates and Steve Greenberg of Greenberg Public Relations were key players in

---

[*] Silver was originally sentenced to 12 years and a $7 million fine, which were both lowered on appeal.

working with us in our quest for 50 states. As promised, Governor Cuomo signed the bill into law in a ceremony in April 2016. With the last domino to fall, we became legalized everywhere in America. The nearly 10-year odyssey had come to a victorious end. We had been validated. The map back at my office was a shining, triumphant green, from coast to glorious coast.

■ ■ ■

Madison Square Garden, in the heart of New York City, is considered the mecca of basketball, but it was also boxing's first capital back in the 1940s and 1950s. Before the sport took root in Las Vegas, New York City was the place to be for fighters and where iconic bouts like Joe Louis-Rocky Marciano took place, and in later years, Ali-Frazier I and II. It's where the Knicks and Rangers both won championships, where celebrities filled the front row, and where the biggest stars in the world came to perform for adoring crowds. The old lyric about being able to make it anywhere if you could make there applied to us as well.

In November 2016, UFC held its first event at The Garden. That whole week felt like a celebration and a victory lap, so I soaked up every minute. On Friday at the weigh-in, I walked through the stone bowels of the arena. My heart was pumping. I could sense the energy and feel the vibration of the crowd above me. When I came out of the tunnel, it was a sight: The Garden was full—for the weigh-in! A crowd of that size came to watch men and women stand on a scale. It was a testament to the immense anticipation, the sport's popularity, and the draw of the fighters. All that work had paid off, and I was beaming.

There were three title fights on that card. The most we'd ever had on one night. The main event would be featherweight champion Conor McGregor, UFC's biggest star, going up against lightweight champion Eddie Alvarez. McGregor was looking to be the first fighter in history to hold two belts simultaneously. So, there was a built-in narrative and anticipation about his quest on top of everything else. On Saturday, the crowd for the fight made the weigh-in fans look like an opera crowd. They were high-energy, vocal, and clearly invested. This was their sport, they felt personal about it, and they showed up in droves. They, too, understood the celebratory aspect of UFC's first night in The Garden. The $20 million gate broke records. It was the biggest gate in the arena's history for an event of any kind. On Monday, there would be more work on my desk, but we had accomplished the thing I was brought on board to do. Despite the politicking, the aggravation, the exhaustion, the nearly 10-year battle, I couldn't stop smiling.*

A new spin on the familiar Peanuts cartoon given to me by one of UFC's graphic artists.

---

* *Peanuts* picture needs to be scanned. A pic from the MSG night would be good too.

CHAPTER TWELVE

■ ■ ■

Fight Week

UFC events happen on one night, but they aren't created in one night. For those of us behind the scenes, fight night is the culmination of a two- to three-month process. To ensure that an event goes off without a hitch—or as few hitches as possible—we have to lay the groundwork well in advance. UFC's matchmakers work with Dana to set up the fights around six to eight weeks in advance. Match-ups are especially difficult in MMA because fighters come from so many different disciplines (boxing, wrestling, kickboxing, jiu-jitsu), but that is what adds variety into the bloodstream of the sport. The various specialties and backgrounds, along with the international influences, blend together in a way that's more reflective of the 21st Century world. When people talk about MMA being the sport of the future, this is why. In addition, technology has allowed for extensive breakdowns of fighters' moves, statistics, strengths, and weaknesses, which helps matchmakers and gives certain fans, the sabermetrics crowd, another element to enjoy. It takes combat sports beyond the somewhat dated and one-dimensional realm of win-loss records. The complex statistics are there for those interested in the granular detail, but the sport is also simple enough for a newcomer to pick up right away.

MMA's accessibility works in its favor: the sport is recognizable to people who've never even seen a match before. "Most people have never engaged in a fight with regular boxing rules," Extreme Fighting pioneer Donald Zuckerman said. "But at one time or another, even if it was only on the playground in grade school, virtually everyone has engaged in some form of fighting."[31] In recent years MMA and karate gyms have become regular features of cities and suburbs, catering to men, women, young children, amateurs, workout enthusiasts, and even seniors. Unless you know where the boxing gyms are in a city, they're hard to find, but you'll see storefront karate, jiu-jitsu, and MMA studios all over.

Another reason for UFC's popularity is that the larger structure of UFC is easy to grasp. There is a single belt for each weight division (and gender), and that's it. For all of professional boxing's popularity, I don't know anyone who enjoys the fact that there's multiple sanctioning bodies, each giving out a different belt. It makes it harder for the casual fan to follow, which can kill a sport's growth. I consider myself a knowledgeable boxing fan, and it's even hard for to me to name all the heavyweight champions. No fighting promotion comes close to UFC's reach. Plus, within UFC, there are not independent promoters looking out for only their fighter's record, interest, or image. Ultimately, it's about the strongest match-up, what the fans want to see, and what's best for the sport.

UFC's matchmakers have an incredibly tough job, probably second behind the fighters themselves. They deal with fighters all over the world and are getting messages 24 hours a day regarding injuries, visa problems, and all the logistics of putting a fight together. Pre-eminent matchmaker Joe Silva retired in 2016, and he passed his matchmaking torch to Sean Shelby and Mick Maynard.

Not only do they have to find suitable fighters from divergent backgrounds and weigh the complex factors that make for a good fight, but they also have to be quick on their feet. MMA fighters frequently get injured while training, so matchmakers often need to find available and appropriate substitutes on short notice. It can be a logistical nightmare, especially for high-profile fights for which fans are expecting a certain caliber of match-up. In June 2015, the match between Conor McGregor and featherweight champ Jose Aldo was postponed when Aldo fractured a rib a few days before the event. Conor still wanted to fight—he's a gamer—so Chad Mendes ably stepped in. I'm in awe of these fighters. Very few people on earth would (or could) step into the Octagon with Conor McGregor in front of the world on fewer than one week's notice.*

Once the match-ups and venue are set, I act as the liaison between UFC and that state's athletic commission, if one exists. In Nevada, I work closely with Bob Bennett, a former Marine and boxing judge who is now Executive Director of the NSAC, my previous job. Bob is an old-school guy, tough but friendly, with a pronounced New York accent and a no-nonsense manner. He and I discuss judges, referees, medicals, weigh-in times, any possible issues—all the details that allow fight week to run smoothly. In other states, I link up with Bob's counterparts. If there is not a commission, we "self-regulate," which means we do it all ourselves, building up the infrastructure from scratch.

UFC depends on the health and safety of its fighters, the talent who make the sport possible. We ensure, first and foremost, that our fighters are protected. We have opened the UFC Performance Institute at our headquarters in Las Vegas to work with the fighters on nutrition, weight training, injury rehabilitation, and safely cutting weight. There are medical and emergency personnel, as well as ambulances, on site and ready at all UFC events. Local hospitals are prepped in advance, and all fighters are given rigorous pre- and post-fight monitoring. We use USADA, an independent drug testing company, that tests around the clock for stimulants and illegal performance-enhancing drugs (PEDs). UFC also has its own medical consultant who travels to most fights to supplement local doctors.

---

* On top of everything, McGregor is also left-handed, which throws off most fighters.

With advances in medicine, science, and technology, we owe it to our fighters to be on top of everything. Having lost seven fighters on my watch during my days with the commission, I treat this with the gravity it deserves. Only when these precautions are put in place can you truly enjoy the fight, which is what I had been saying on "Larry King Live" all those years ago.

Certain required medical tests and fight rules vary from state to state, which is something of a headache. Every time we schedule a fight, I have to ask, "What medical tests are you asking for?" and "Are you using the newest version of the Unified Rules of MMA?" Some rules—like the grounded opponent rule—change depending on the venue. If a fighter is "grounded," he or she can't be kneed or kicked in the head. In some states, fighters are allowed to put a hand down to make themselves grounded, while in other states they need both hands down. It's a nightmare for announcers, analysts, judges, and especially fighters—not to mention confusing for the fans. I'd love to see that streamlined, as there's no practical reason for this. It's just politics.

When we're hosting an event in a location for the first time (or for the first time in a long time), I often fly out there in advance to be an ambassador for UFC. In the midwest or on the east coast, I meet the commission and the team at the venue and emphasize: *This will be different from a boxing match.* I try to set the table, prepare them for what to expect, what problems might arise, and answer their questions. The last thing I want is to find out the day of the fight that something essential is not in place.

Referees play an outsized role in MMA, so their training, performance, and selection are hugely important. A referee's decision to stop a fight—they have to physically step in between the fighters at just the right moment—needs to be correct, swift, and on time. Too early is unfair and too late is dangerous. In my job as Vice President of Regulatory Affairs, I've found that every state in the U.S. (and most places overseas) thinks it has the best officials. I politely tell them that we'd like to supplement them with some world-class referees.

Their guys may know their stuff, but when you put them before 10,000 people, can they handle it? It's not because of their skills, but simply their lack of experience. Most officials are not accustomed to this level of attention or scrutiny that comes with an international sporting event. As a former sports official, I know the environment has an impact on officials, psychologically and physiologically. The size of the arena, the noise of the crowd, the cameras, the reach of the broadcast, the stakes of the game, even the celebrities in the audience—it all affects the competitors, so why wouldn't it affect the officials? They're trained, unbiased professionals with years of experience, but they're not robots.

Officiating is a thankless job in which you're in a no-win situation. No one ever likes you, and you never can get a crowd on your side. The best you can do is not screw up. As I've said before, a good official is one you don't notice. That's a tough circumstance for anyone. Then throw in two fighters, whose health and safety is in your hands, and maybe then people can begin to understand the pressure involved in the job.

In my football officiating days, I had friends who were long-time college and NFL referees, and they'd talk about how once the ball is kicked, it's like any other game. That had been true for me—until I called a game at Notre Dame. Knowing the history of *that* school and *that* stadium (before leaving home I watched "Rudy"), being on *that* field with the leprechaun running around and the crowd noise like a wave of sound, it certainly *was not* like any other game. Notre Dame head coach Charlie Weis said, "Listen, I'm going to yell and talk at you, but don't take it personally." As line judge, one my pre-game duties was to bring the home team out for the coin flip, and there is a sign that all the Notre Dame players touch when they are going out to the field. It says, "Play Like a Champion Today." I touched the sign, too.

At kick off, I had tears in my eyes. It was one of the few times I was really nervous, though my excitement, surrounded by almost 80,000 screaming Fighting Irish fans and 75 years of tradition. It was the one time I felt intimidated. To this day, it was the most thrilling officiating experience of my life, better than any bowl game I've worked. But it also taught me what it's like in the belly of the beast. The atmosphere, the crowd, the stakes, the pressure, and the audience *do* come into play. An experienced referee learns over time to lower the volume on those things and ultimately how to block them out. However, those accustomed to a crowd of 1,500 people, will not be able to ignore 10,000. You don't know until you're in it. On that aspect alone, it's similar to the fighters themselves. We can't afford to learn in the middle of a major fight that they can't handle the job.

As in boxing, the outcome of a fight is not always an objective fact, so judges also play an outsized role. Anyone who regularly watches MMA can judge maybe 80 percent of the rounds. What differentiates an average judge from a professional is the other 20 percent, the close ones. The five-minute rounds require extended focus and concentration. Judges have to mentally track the round's entire sequence, retain their memory of the opening minute and balance it in their minds with the final minute, while also understanding how to properly evaluate each move, hit, and takedown.

In grappling matches, judges have to watch much more closely (they have personal video monitors) and they have to *know* what they're watching. It's not common sense, and impressions can be deceiving. As I discovered during my early days learning MMA, the fighter on the bottom may very well be in control. Dana once said his criteria for who wins an MMA fight is simple: *Who has done the most damage?* It's one of the things that is hard to quantify, but after hundreds and hundreds of fights, he knows it when he sees it, as do I.

No matter the opponent, there is no such thing as an easy fight. What happens in the Octagon is really just the tip of a deeply set iceberg. There are thousands of hours of "off-stage" work that the fighters have to do to be competitive professionals. At the weigh-in, you get a sense of how difficult training is, especially the strenuous process of maintaining and cutting weight. During the final week of training, their intensity of work increases while their calories decrease, which does a number on them. As MMA fighters mature, it becomes that much more difficult for them to stay in shape year-around (there is no offseason in MMA) and to lose weight before a fight. Those who stay in MMA past their peak age are some of the most dedicated athletes in the world.

On the Tuesday of a Saturday fight week, the fighters flood from various points in the world to the host city, drinking alkaline or denatured water by the gallon. This is a process called "water loading," which biologically makes it easier for them to cut water weight before Friday's weigh-in. Some fighters drop as much as 20 pounds between Tuesday and Friday. Then, after the weigh-in, they put almost all of the weight back on. Though some with wrestling backgrounds are used to it, it's an arduous process, and no one likes doing it. But it's all part of the sport.

On a Friday morning in March 2020, I passed through the rattling morning noise of the New York-New York Hotel & Casino in Las Vegas and went up the escalator to the carpeted hallways of the private conference rooms. Those who come to Las Vegas on business spend their days in these rooms, but that day they were empty except for us. Passing through a phalanx of security, I traded hellos and good mornings with familiar faces before I reached the room at the end the hall. I stepped in and took a seat at the fold-out chair right by the door. A scale was set up in front of a large UFC banner under two industrial grade square lights, and a slew of media members were crunched together in vinyl chairs—bloggers, newspaper writers, online media, television reporters, balancing their coffees, with their boom mics and tripods piled on top of each other with their phones and laptops. ESPN had a mini production in the corner, and Ariel Helwani and Brett Okamoto were doing a stand-up spot to camera among a sophisticated array of lights, cameras, and computer equipment.

Behind the rows of press was a black cordon rope where some fans, young and old, who had gotten up early after a night in Las Vegas, congregated to get a glimpse of their favorites. It has been many decades since I had come out to see Sonny Liston at the Thunderbird Hotel to pose, train, and interact with fans, but the essence was the same. Some things just don't change.

I said hello to Bob Bennett, dressed head-to-toe in black from his turtleneck to his sneakers. Bob was running the show that morning, which meant he was personally weighing the fighters, while UFC's Vice President of Operations Amber Bowen kept track and announced the fighters' names as they came out from the back room. As they got ready to start, Reed Harris took a seat next to me. Reed, a silver-haired former fighter in an impressive gray suit, was the Senior Vice President of Athlete Development. Once a real estate developer, Reed was teaching taekwondo as a hobby when he met the iconic fighter Chuck Liddell, with whom he traded house-hunting assistance for jiu-jitsu lessons. Reed later started WEC (World Extreme Cagefighting), which was sold to UFC in 2006. His role was to help fighters with everything from endorsement deals to retirement plans. UFC helps fighters train, pays for their medical bills, and after they retire, employs many of them who want to come work for the organization. Though UFC has grown considerably, it still retains the feel of a community, a family even.

I make a point to attend as many as weigh-ins as I can. Even after many hundreds, they still carry that sense of excitement for me. When I ran the weigh-ins myself, especially for the iconic fighters, my blood would get pumping when they stepped on that scale. It's like the first scene of a movie or the first note of a rock song. The weigh-in is about the elemental questions and answers: who and what and if and how much. Unlike the ceremonial weigh-in that happened later that day at the arena, in front of crowds with Dana and Joe Rogan and blasting music, this one was more casual. There were private conversations, friendly joking, and a noticeable camaraderie among the fighters, media, and larger community.

Along with the small crowd in a back, a few journalists shouted out the names of fighters as they entered. Amber introduced the fighters, who stepped out barefoot from the back room and stripped down to their underwear. Some brushed their hair before they stepped on, knowing the cameras would be firing away. After Bob called out their weight and flicked the metal piece back with a clang, the fighters flexed and posed before exiting with their coach or trainer.

Fighters have to make weight inside the two-hour window between 9 a.m. and 11 a.m., and the suspense arises from those who wait until the last minute. There are always a few fighters with no weight concerns who sleep in, especially if they've flown west and are trying to reset their schedule. Plenty of athletes, from basketball to baseball players, have strange eating and sleep schedules because they need to peak in prime time. Others show up at 9 a.m. on the dot to get it out of the way. After they're weighed in, they can start drinking water again, eating normally, and getting prepared for the fight. They may talk strategy with their coaches or just take it easy. UFC's doctors stay in the hotel with the fighters and are on call for them in case there are any medical problems. UFC's safety record is very important and considering the intense level of hand-to-hand combat, there's not as much serious injury as you'd think, as compared to professional football or even boxing.

Middleweight champion Israel Adesanya—the headliner for the next night's fight—was there 9 a.m. on the dot. (He's practically waiting for us.) A champion from Nigeria, he was lean and tall, a fluid kickboxing machine who went by the moniker "The Last Stylebender." Adesanya was undefeated, and his challenger was the Cuban-born Yoel Romero. Romero was a veteran at age 42, though he had the body and stamina of someone half his age. He was a former wrestler who could grapple with the best of them. The two fighters' body types, approaches, and fighting styles were so different, which would make either a really fascinating fight or a disaster. We had no idea what to expect, which added a layer of excitement. Romero was nowhere to be seen at that moment. He was likely still at the UFC Performance Institute and was not alone. During this two-hour window, many fighters were there, on bikes or in saunas, cutting weight until the last minute.

At 10:50 a.m., there was tension in the room as Romero entered wearing nothing but a towel around his waist. He is a tank of a man, "built like a granite sculpture," as one writer vividly put it.[32] Yoel knew he was close enough to the weight cut off that he'd have to step onto the scale wearing nothing but a UFC towel shielding his body. Often, we used a large black hoop—there was one earlier for the female fighters—but Amber told me it had gone missing.

Bob leaned in front of the scale and recited his weight. "185."

An exhale passed through the crowd. The title fight would go on. Yoel clapped his hands together and yelled, "How many years!?" Then he slapped his bare chest a few times. "How many years?!" he yelled again. Yoel stepped off in a hurry, likely relieved to have made it on time and underweight, but Amber waved him back on the scale for photos. He put his shorts back on and then froze for the media, looked up and pointed at sky in a semi-religious pose. There was a brief cheer as he exited. The crowd in the back remained; they were still waiting to get a glimpse of their favorite fighter.

"Zhang Weili," Amber announced. A chorus of whoops rose from the press rows.

"Weili," they called out to her. "Let's go, champ! Looking good, champ!" Zhang Weili, the female strawweight champion, was UFC's first title holder from East Asia. She was an absolute superstar back home in China, where her fights got millions of views and where she was the face of the sport. Physically she was quite small; if you passed her on the street, you'd have no idea much damage she could do. Devastating and quick-acting, Weili lost her first professional fight in 2013, but she hadn't lost since. She easily made weight on this morning, and the fans by the back wall let out a collective cheer.

It was her challenger, Joanna Jędrzejczyk, who received the biggest greeting of the morning. Joanna, a former champion out of Poland, was the underdog who some people thought had the chance for an upset. She tied her hair up on top of her head and stepped onto the scale, confidently making a No. 1 sign with her index finger. After Bob called out her weight, "115." the crowd in the back erupted.

Though Weili was the champion, Joanna was the fan favorite. By the end of that fight, everyone knew them both.

In the past 10 years, UFC has come a long way in bringing female fighters onto an equal playing field with men. It's balanced in a way that I believe is unmatched in any other professional sport. But that wasn't always the case. There have been a few UFC fighters through the years who rose to such stardom that they transformed the sport. The entire industry then rode their wave into mainstream popularity. That's what happened with Ronda Rousey.

In 2011, UFC bought an MMA promotion out of San Jose named Strikeforce, which came with some very impressive fighters, none more so than the women's bantamweight champion, "Rowdy" Ronda Rousey. From a young age, Ronda was taken under the wing of some of the most iconic MMA coaches, who all could tell how special she was going to be. Her mother was a former judo champion and was a major influence on her. At age 17, Ronda took home the Olympic bronze in judo. She was the first American woman to medal and the youngest judoka to ever compete. She dominated with her signature armbar move in which she got her opponents on the ground and essentially bent their arms back into submission. She could get into that position in a blink, and no one could get out of it.

At one time, cornered by a paparazzi camera, Dana had said he was never going to allow women to fight in UFC. Ronda changed his mind; she changed a lot of people's minds. In March 2012, after months of trading barbs in the press, Ronda and Miesha Tate, a former state wrestling champion, fought for the Strikeforce women's bantamweight belt in title in Columbus, Ohio. I took in the match with Dana and other UFC executives.

As accomplished as Tate was, Ronda got her to submit to the armbar before the end of the first round. After getting the victory, Ronda refused to shake Tate's hand. Tate had apparently said something about Ronda's family, and Ronda said she wasn't going to pretend and that she wasn't fake. This only made her more popular. Once Dana saw Ronda fight, he admitted his error. A few months later after another win, she went to Dana, and asked him, "Do you see what I can bring?"

He did. We all did. I saw her fight Sarah Kaufman in San Diego a few months later, and I was just awed, watching her get Kaufman to submit in the armbar in less than a minute. Rousey was so impressive that night, and I could see she was special—the way she carried herself, her self-assurance, and her charisma. A few years later, when she came to Albany to help us lobby for the legalization of MMA, I saw those same qualities that made her unique. Everyone just responded to her.

Less than a year later, UFC dissolved Strikeforce and brought over all of its remaining roster. Dana was so impressed with Ronda that he made her first fight—the first ever women's UFC fight—the main event on the card at UFC 157. In Anaheim, Ronda's appeal sold out the 15,000-seat arena, lured a huge Pay-Per-View audience, and she put on an incredible display against Liz Carmouche. By the time the referee raised her arm in victory, Ronda was a legitimate star. "A gigantic cultural moment," announcer Joe Rogan called it. For her next six fights, Ronda was unstoppable. No one could get out of the first round against her. The media converged on her, spectators cheered her name, and new fans flocked to the sport.

A few years later, Ronda was in such demand—commercials, advertisements, charities, public speaking gigs, television, movies, video games—that fighting almost became secondary. Her skill and natural charisma transcended the sport, and she became an industry of her own. She retired soon after losing her title and spent a couple of years as a big draw in professional wrestling (WWE) before retiring in 2019 to start a family with her husband, former fighter Travis Browne. I'm happy for her. She worked hard for the recognition, and she remains a superb role model for everyone, men and women.

MMA always had a contingent of female fight fans, but after Ronda, there was a visible spike in that audience. We could see it in the data and with our own eyes at the events. Now, there is rarely an event without women on the card. UFC has more than 100 female fighters across four weight divisions. It has come a long way since Dana thought there wouldn't be enough female fighters to fill just one weight class. A previous generation tried to argue that men don't want to see women fight, but that's been proven wrong many million times over.

While attempting to persuade state legislators to legalize MMA, I held up UFC's equal treatment of women as a rarity in professional sports. The rules of the fight are the same. The number of rounds and the length of those rounds are the same. The fighters are paid according to the same criteria: when they sell tickets and bring viewers, women get paid what men get paid. One of my arguments against boxing is that the women's two-minute rounds should be extended to three minutes, just like the men's rounds. It makes no sense. In MMA, if women can fight for five-minute rounds, there is no reason why women in boxing shouldn't fight for three.

People might think of MMA as a violent throwback, but in so many ways it is a progressive institution in its values, personnel, and execution. A 2018 bantamweight title match in Brazil was the first to feature two female fighters (Amanda Nunes vs Raquel Pennington) who were both in relationships with other female fighters. Former fighter and current analyst Dan Hardy called the historic event "a celebration all-around for the [LGBTQ] community."[33] Meanwhile, the female audience has been steadily growing, and with each UFC event, we see far more couples, bachelorette parties, and girls' nights out. Many women fighters have followed in her footsteps, but we have Ronda to thank for getting the ball rolling. It doesn't matter your age, gender, or background, everyone just wants to see a good fight.

■ ■ ■

One Saturday, I arrived at T-Mobile Arena in the mid-afternoon, about an hour before the first fight. I checked in with the television production team to let them know I was there. Occasionally they would ask me questions on the broadcast through my headset. One time, Greg Hardy used an inhaler in his corner between rounds, and broadcaster John Anik asked me if it was legal. "Completely illegal," I responded. "No question about it." It's performance enhancing, and I was surprised the corner guys didn't know. I couldn't imagine they thought we wouldn't notice.

A member of the Nevada commission staff found me and passed along the referee and judge assignments, along with last-minute changes. I wandered over to the opposite end of the Octagon to chat with members of the press in media row. Then I found NSAC Executive Director Bob Bennett and spoke to him briefly. I had been in his position, and I knew what it was like before fight night unfolds. You want it to go off without a hitch and for it to end without any problems or controversy. After wishing him luck, I took my seat at the Octagon in front of the sound board, headset, and a TV monitor labeled RATNER. The Octagon has decidedly more space than a boxing ring—it looks huge up close when it's empty—which gives more runway for fighters to build up speed to strike, to takedown an opponent, or even to jump on their back. Since there are no corners, it's also harder to be pinned or trapped by the Octagon itself.

The arena's seats were nowhere near filled, especially not the fold-out chairs on the floor, reserved for VIPs and staff, but the fights were set to begin. The early fights are called "preliminary," but they have as much potential as the main event. There's possibility and surprise, the chance for the night's best fight. Sometimes, we'll see the break out of a new star, and occasionally, the final grasps of a career. The fighters in the prelims are less well known, but they're there for the same reason as the headliners. If anything, they have *more* to prove; they want to move up in status or ranking, gain a following, or make a name for themselves. In addition, fighters who are in the "Fight of the Night" or give the "Performance of the Night" earn a $50,000 bonus on top of their contractual purse. Each fight is an opportunity, and no one steps into the Octagon to phone it in. It's just not possible.

Since the crowd sounds were low and scattered, at the prelims, you could hear the added intimacy of stomps and slaps and thuds.* You could hear family and friends in the crowd whose shouts told you that, to them, *this* was the main event. Without crowd noise, you could hear the coaches clearly, and it was like being inside a football huddle or a basketball timeout. The liveness of a UFC fight is a palpable thing. The heightened feel of something happening in front of you, unscripted, gets its hooks in you and doesn't let go.

As the seats filled up, there was an electricity in the air, a feeling of expectation mixed with apprehension. As the prelims came to an end, the seats started to fill and you could watch each spectator get roped in. If you've ever watched UFC on television, it's interesting, but until you've seen it live, it's hard to describe. It's part sporting event, part skill match, part rock concert, part theater, and part pep rally.

Dana, wearing an open-collared shirt and jacket, traveled through the crowd like the town mayor. Fans, celebrities, and kids all wanted to take pictures with him and talk, and he obliged. One thing that impresses me about Dana—and I've seen it many times—is he will sign every autograph and take every picture, even if it means being late or even holding up a plane. He never turns anyone down. Most athletes won't even do that, much less someone who has to run the entire promotion. He's the face of UFC, and he knows his behavior matters. There's nothing worse than a kid remembering that his hero didn't sign his autograph. We encourage the fighters to engage with the fans, and Dana models that behavior.

Dana acts and thinks like a fan, which affects the tenor of everything at UFC. He's a straightforward guy who's not much for

---

* During the Covid-19 crisis of 2020, when UFC events had no crowds, viewers on TV got that same experience of hearing the coaches yelling, the time calls, the heavy breathing, and the Octagon's floor shaking. I was at some of those fights, and you could really hear everything. The fighters could even hear the announcers.

corporate speak or hedging. What you see is what you get. How he is at press conferences and fights is how he is around the office, on conference calls, and in meetings. He's not afraid to speak his mind or say what a fan will say. When there's a bad decision, he'll admit it. When a fight disappoints, he'll say so. When a fighter's conduct crosses the line, he'll call them out. When a fight reaches a highpoint, he'll jump out of his seat in excitement, cheer and yell and applaud along with the rest of the crowd.

The five-minute rounds in MMA make it unique in combat sports. You can't really hide, play possum, or run out the clock. The rounds are long enough to allow the pendulum of the fight to completely swing the other way. Inside one round, a story can be set up, build, peak, and conclude. There's not just varieties between fights, there's variety *inside* the fights themselves. In a moment, a striker's duel can become a grappling match that can become a kickboxing contest. Though their fight plans are often mapped out in advance, a fighter will improvise in order to turn the fight into something else. This makes MMA more like chess, with strategic thinking that's focused on multiple moves ahead. A fighter may let an opponent keep it a boxing match in order tire him or her out; then as exhaustion sets in, the fighter will take over and turn it into a ground game, if they can handle their own. Then they lead the fight back to the feet to go for the knockout. As exhaustion sets in, and strategy starts to fade, you'll see the trading of punches. If a knockout appears close, the noise of the crowd goes up like a crest of a wave.

The round ends with the piercing sound of the airhorn—rather than the classic boxing bell—which itself highlights the difference between the two sports. An airhorn is more raucous, and it's a fan's noise, a celebratory noise. Fan engagement is a huge part of the fight, and the crowd knows it. They will express dissatisfaction with a fighter, fight, or official by chanting less-than-kind words or holding their lit phones up in the air in what looks like a swarm of fireflies.

The audience has changed considerably from UFC's early days. Spectators are now a mix of white-collared folk in suits to t-shirted and tattooed working-class people, from Southern rural areas to Northern urban ones, to suburban kids and their parents, to young couples, to wrestling fans. When Brock Lesnar or CM Punk, former popular wrestlers, came over to compete in MMA, they brought a large contingent of wrestling fans with them. There is some crossover—wrestling is sports entertainment—but MMA and UFC are, as the slogan says, "As real as it gets."

As the night progressed and the lights went down, I saw less of the crowd but could hear more of them. Around 7 p.m., when the stadium was at capacity and the floor started to shake, the vibration ran through my body. The Octagon became more centralized, like the stage of a concert. It became too loud to have conversations and too dark to do anything but focus on the match. The light show moved in sync to the music, which was turned up to full volume. At my favorite point of the night, right before the main card started, the elaborate sound system went into The Who's "Baba O'Reilly." When its opening synthesizer refrain got drowned out by the crash of guitar and drums, I felt young again. There was no place I'd rather be.

Something fascinating about MMA is that—unlike just about every other sport—you'll sometimes see a crowd decide to switch allegiance during a fight. A fighter can actually win over the crowd. (Under no circumstances will Yankees fans start pulling for the Red Sox.) It's a type of respect, a recognition of heart and talent. Of course, there are hometown favorites, and the crowd will battle back and forth with each other, but you'll also see a mass conversion over to certain fighters if their performance is impressive enough.

Both men's and women's title fights that night went the distance. There wasn't much action in the Adesanya-Romero fight. Both were hesitant to play each other's game, and the fans let us hear about it, doing that firefly thing with their phones. Their styles were just too different and neither wanted to give an inch, so they stayed conservative through five rounds. It was disappointing, and Dana later said so at the post-fight press conference. That's why people love him.

However, the women's title match between Weili Zhang and Joanna Jędrzejczyk more than made up for it. Joanna walked out to Aerosmith ("Dream On"), while the champ walked out to a deep red light show, a Chinese song on the sound system, and her home country flag displayed on the jumbotron. It was a fight for the ages—one the best I've ever seen. Weili was a superstar, but Joanna held her own. Both fighters took serious blows to the face, and by the fifth round, they both looked like they had been through hell. The crowd rode the waves as each fighter went for the knockout as time ran down. Then came the decision, with Bruce Buffer announcing the winner in his inimitable stye. "Winner annnnnnnnnnnnnnnnd..." He built up the suspense because the next word, either "still" or "new," would reveal who won. When he said "still," a roar passed through the crowd. Weili kept her belt, but it was no walk in the park. She absolutely had to earn it.

By the time the crowd filtered out into the street and casinos after 10 p.m., they were coming down from a six-hour high. Many were amped up and want to keep the night going. However, I was ready to call it a night. The fresh air felt good on my face, and as I was just about as happy as I get. No serious injury, no controversy, and I knew I would be able ease into my Monday morning without too much crashing down on me.

Then we'd do it all over again.

CHAPTER THIRTEEN

■ ■ ■

Notorious

In 2013, I traveled with UFC to Sweden for an event at Ericsson Globe, a stadium in Stockholm which looks like a futuristic space station or maybe a giant golf ball. It was the UFC debut of a 24-year-old Irish fighter who was getting a great deal of hype. Conor McGregor had been dominating fights in Cage Warriors, a British fighting promotion, where he was both featherweight and lightweight champion at the same time. McGregor was a true knockout artist (11 of his 12 wins were KOs), who are always fan favorites. That night, McGregor was a promising upstart fighter on the undercard, the fourth fight of the night against Marcus Brimage.

Conor had his head shaved on the sides and fewer tattoos than he does now, but his swagger and showmanship was a cut above everyone else that evening. He was awarded a "Performance of the Night" bonus for knocking out Brimage in just 67 seconds. I met him afterward, and he spoke about being "on the dole"—social welfare—and how the bonus money meant a great deal to him. I don't think anyone knew how good or how big Conor would become, but we knew he possessed star quality from day one. He carried a big personality outside the Octagon and showed complete domination within it. After that impressive debut, it was like he shot out of a rocket. His career exploded that fast.

Conor dominated the UFC featherweight division and was scheduled to fight lightweight champion Jose Aldo in June 2015. The fight was delayed six months because of the champion's broken rib, but in December, the two finally met in the Octagon. Aldo had been undefeated for 10 years and was widely considered the best "pound-for-pound" fighter in the world. In a blink, it was over; Conor knocked him out in 13 seconds. It was no fluke. McGregor had accumulated so many first round knockouts—so quickly—that the only fighter comparable to him was Tyson. He was like a 21st Century MMA version of Iron Mike.

I've gotten to know Conor through the years. I've watched him train and have been there in private when it's just him, his fiancée Dee, and his tight circle of people. Away from it all, one-on-one, he's just a regular guy. Most fighters are. You just have to catch them away from their entourage, the fans, or a camera. Some of the more outrageous stuff Conor says and does in public is about self-promotion, ticket sales and Pay-Per-View buys. Ronda did the same thing. He understands that he has the sport on his back. UFC has never had a bigger star. Whether he's fighting or not, Conor is the name on everyone's lips.

So, it didn't seem like too much of a leap when he started talking about getting into the boxing ring with the undefeated welterweight champion of the world, the greatest boxer of his generation, Floyd Mayweather Jr. It seemed too fantastic a prospect to pass up, so both sides went to work to make it happen.

The fight between Mayweather and McGregor was scheduled for August 2017. In the months beforehand, Conor trained at the UFC Performance Institute every day where we brought in a regulation boxing ring. Conor worked as hard as any athlete I've ever seen: doing cardio, working the bag, practicing footwork, and going through many sparring partners, including former fighter Paulie Malignaggi. There was a bit of controversy after photos came out of their sparring match, with Conor saying he knocked Paulie down, and Paulie claiming he was pushed. It got heated, and Paulie ended up leaving Conor's camp. Dana later posted a video on Instagram which verified Conor's version. There's no shame in getting knocked down by McGregor. He has some heavy hands, and he's proven it in MMA. The question was whether or not it would translate to boxing. At first, I was not so sure.

But I was impressed after sitting with his people, like his manager Audie Attar and trainer John Cavanaugh, watching Conor train and spar. I felt like he had a good chance. He was obviously the underdog, which was rare for him. Not only was he not a professional boxer, but he was going up against the best, the undefeated champ, someone used to fighting 12 three-minute rounds, instead of MMA's five five-minute rounds. There was just no way that Conor could beat Mayweather in the stamina game. His best shot was a knockout in one of the early rounds. McGregor would have to go for it early or risk losing an endurance competition.

There are Sports Page fights, and then there are Front Page fights. Mayweather-McGregor was the latter, and the atmosphere the week of the fight reminded me of when Tyson would come to town in his peak. It just enveloped Las Vegas, took over the city for the weekend, and no one could talk about anything else. All the sports and gambling outlets were on top of it, and I wondered if the match could possibly live up to the hype.

The event sold out, with a $50 million gate. More than six million homes and businesses around the world bought the fight. It was the most talked about sporting event of the year, like a combat sports version of the Super Bowl. The idea behind the fight, pitting the two best in their respective sports against each other, was reminiscent of Rorion Gracie's original idea behind UFC: putting fighters from different disciplines against each other to see who would be left standing.

On fight night, after I finished watching Floyd's hands being wrapped in his dressing room, the referee came in. Robert Byrd, a longtime veteran who I knew well from my time at the commission, came in to brief Floyd and his team. Floyd asked him to make sure there was no hitting in the back of the head, what are known as rabbit punches, but the champ otherwise seemed unfazed. As long as his opponent followed the rules, Floyd appeared confident in a victory.

About 10 minutes before the fighters walked, I found my seat with my son Heiden to take in what might become the most watched fight in the history of the world. McGregor came out shirtless with the tricolor Irish flag draped over his shoulders and one of his entourage holding up his UFC belt. Floyd came out almost dancing, wearing a sequined black outfit with zippers and a full ski mask covering his face.

During the referee's instructions, Byrd kept his focus on Conor, emphasizing what he was not allowed to do in the boxing ring. There had been some general concern that McGregor might revert to an MMA move, perhaps use his feet or throw Floyd down. Clearly Byrd was concerned about it, too. The referee really didn't take his eyes off Conor during the instructions. It brought a home/visitor dynamic to the fight, though the crowd seemed split about half and half between who they were rooting for.

There's a special feeling when the bell rings to start a fight, a great anticipation in the air, like a mass inhale waiting to breathe out. Looking over, I could see Dana seemed a little nervous. I knew I couldn't root for Conor—I'm always a regulator first—but I just wanted him to be competitive. The last thing we needed was a first-round knockout, which would have tagged the event as a "money grab" that never should have happened.

From the opening bell, Conor came out swinging. He hit Floyd with a solid uppercut, which didn't seem to bother the champ at all, though it did get Conor's juices flowing. He taunted Floyd a little, mixed it up, even put his hands behind his back at one point. At the end of the first round, I could feel the level of excitement lift as people saw this was going to be for real. Conor's strong early performance silenced his doubters and let everyone know this was no stunt.

Conor also had the advantage of being a lefty, a southpaw in the parlance, who gave even the best fighters trouble. The next few rounds, he held his own, looking like a real boxer. But Floyd was brilliant, and as the fight went on, his experience and training just took over. Floyd moved quickly and gradually let Conor—who was used to shorter fights—gas himself out. The longer the fight went, the more it fell in Floyd's favor. As Conor's exhaustion set in during the later rounds, and Floyd's punches got more accurate, the tide visibly turned. When Byrd stopped the fight in the tenth round, it was the right call. Conor was having trouble keeping his hands up, and Floyd was hitting him at will.

It turned out to be a win for everybody. It was a better fight than people expected and a windfall for all concerned. Conor and Floyd embraced, and despite all the taunting and press conference antics, they seemed to have mutual respect for each other. The end result was a testament to Floyd, who will forever be a great champion. But it was also a huge validation for Conor, who stepped into a different sport and took the champion to 10 rounds. I can't imagine anyone else in the world that would be willing or able to do that.

McGregor is so confident that he almost immediately started talking about a rematch; he really thinks he can beat him. Then I heard that Floyd was talking about coming into MMA, which just didn't seem possible. At least Conor had once been an amateur boxer and had a punching background. I don't see a 40-something Floyd learning wrestling and jiu-jitsu. In the Octagon, the fight is inevitably going to go to the ground; gravity and momentum just take it there. No matter how hard you hit, an opponent will take that punch and take you down, so you better know what you're doing.

I think UFC has had a positive effect on boxing. Commissions and promoters are removing barriers so that the best boxers can face off because that's what the people want to see: superb athletes at the height of their powers. Of course, with the merging of my past and my present, the night was special on a personal level, too. My first child was boxing, my second was MMA, and I loved both equally. Seeing the two sports successfully come together was a moment I'll always remember, and I got such a rush being part of a boxing match one more time.

I never fully let go of my first love. Boxing writer Thomas Hauser compared boxing to live theater. No matter how many times people have written it off through the years, with the arrival of radio, TV, movies, and the internet, live theater never went away. It's the same with the sweet science. People will always want to go see a boxing match. I will always want to go see one.

Though Mayweather-McGregor felt like a capstone on my previous career, the year before, I was gifted with an incomparable honor that I still can't wrap my head around. The International Boxing Hall of Fame in Canastota, New York voted to enshrine me as a member of their 2016 class. I was to be honored alongside luminaries like the late Hector Camacho, Lupe Pintor, and Hilario Zapata, judge Harold Lederman, boxing writer Jerry Izenberg, and broadcaster Colonel Bob Sheridan. It was something I never expected and an experience I'll never forget.

When I arrived for the weekend, there were already a lot fans around the motel across from the Boxing Hall of Fame. Some even had programs and pictures that they asked me to sign. This was flattering but also uncomfortable. It's very seldom that someone asks me for my autograph. I obliged, and I got a kick out of it.

Later that day, along with the other inductees, the Hall of Fame had me put my hand into a pail of plaster of paris to make a cast of my fist. I couldn't believe it. The next day, Saturday, there was a boxing memorabilia convention that drew a fairly big crowd of collectors and even more fans. At a banquet in nearby Syracuse that night, the new inductees were introduced. Each spoke a few words in front of a room filled with previous Hall of Fame members, including Marvin Hagler, Roberto Duran, Julian Jackson and Jake LaMotta whom Robert DeNiro won the Academy Award for Best Actor by portraying him in "Raging Bull."

My wife Jody and her brother Rick, my children, Heiden (his wife Neena and son Epaph), Mary and David, my sister Susan and her husband Bob, and my cousin Don were all there. They'd supported me through my entire career so it was fitting that I got to share the honor with them. Though my father wasn't a big sports guy, I think he would've gotten a kick out of all this. He was the one who brought us to Las Vegas when I was a boy and took me to my first fight at Cashman Field. My mother Anne passed away in 1992. I remember her on the bleachers at my little league games. She was a gentle soul, and in her final years, we had dinner together once a week. When I found out she had died, I was in Washington, D.C. witnessing my old friend Sig Rogich being sworn in to become U.S. Ambassador to Iceland. My mentor Chuck Minker died the same week. It was so hard to lose both of them so closely together.

On Sunday afternoon in Canastota, there was the traditional Hall of Fame parade, where we all lined up and sat in individual cars marked with our names. Hall of Fame members were in the parade, along with the 2016 inductees and some local politicians, including the mayor. Crowds of waving fans lined the parade route. My daughter Mary rode with me in a car that trailed behind one with Pernell Whitaker inside. As a regulator, I knew I wasn't the one they came to see. It's rare for a regulator to be inducted into the Hall of Fame at all. I received some polite applause, like "golf claps." It was so incredible just to be there in that esteemed company. I never wanted the spotlight; it's not what a good regulator or official should ever seek. But just being honored by the sport, if not feted by the fans, warmed my heart.

I was presented with a Hall of Fame ring with RATNER carved into the gold and there is a plaque permanently on display at their museum. Inside the Hall, the plaque hangs on the wall, alongside reverent displays of robes and shorts and posters and gloves in glass cases, and an old-fashioned Toledo floor scale, with the big circular face and the hand on the clock pointing to the weight. In one of the rooms, there's an old boxing ring from Madison Square Garden, the robes of legendary boxers who fought there hung up along the ropes, its very presence taking me back to the old days.

The whole weekend was like a dream that didn't quite make sense. At the ceremony, I sat onstage alongside my heroes and legends of the sport. It was humbling, being among them: Hagler, Roberto Duran, Sugar Ray Leonard, LaMotta and others. I kept wondering: *What am I doing here? Do I belong in this company?* As writer Jerry Izenberg said in his speech, "We don't bleed; we don't sweat," which was true for regulators as well. Sugar Ray Leonard and the Spinks brothers were there as part of the 1976 U.S. Olympic team, which was honored on the 40th anniversary of their victories in Montreal. Ali had died two weeks earlier, and his absence weighed heavily on everyone that day. "The Greatest" was such a massive figure, not just in boxing but in America. It was hard to believe he was gone.

My former boxing colleagues and friends, like former commission Chairman Dr. James Nave came, as did UFC colleagues like Dana, Lorenzo, Kirk Hendrick and Lawrence Epstein, which was touching and humbling. Lorenzo told me they were planning on it, but I wasn't sure until I saw them. Having my UFC guys fly in from Las Vegas made a great day even more special. I noted that Dana still drew fans in the hard-core boxing crowd, an indication that the worlds are not so separate. When I got to the podium, my whole speech was less than 10 minutes. The nature of my job is not to get attention, and I'm not big on self-promotion. I thanked Chuck Minker because there's no way I'd be up there without his faith in me and his mentorship. He died before he could see what became of the career he helped to launch.

After giving more thanks, I tried to give the audience what they wanted: the controversies. I talked about the "Bite Fight," the "Fan Man" incident, and the Mayweather-Judah brawl. Ironically, my most memorable moments were the ones where things went off the rails. It's funny to think about now, but if Tyson had knocked out Evander after the first bite, I would've been blamed for questioning Mills Lane about his instant disqualification. It probably would have been the end of my career. If I'm remembered by the public, it'll be for those moments. Though I'd hope I'm remembered by my colleagues for my fairness, integrity, and the way I treated everyone I came into contact with—no matter where they fit in the larger scheme of the boxing world.

As a kid growing up going to the fights, I never could have dreamed I'd find myself up on stage among boxing legends. The entire experience was overwhelming and surreal. Boxing was such a huge part of my life, and the whole weekend felt like recognition that I was part of its larger story. That's really all anyone can ask for during a career. I felt as though I had contributed to this historical and beloved institution in my own way. That was enough for me.

Epilogue

■ ■ ■

I never thought in my 70s I'd be traveling the world, hitting all corners of Europe, working in places like Australia, Abu Dhabi, Brazil, Argentina and Russia helping to spread a sport that didn't even exist a few decades ago. Once I joined UFC, I never could've predicted that our fighters would become stars in these places, that their fans would fall in love with the sport, that U.S. fans would embrace them as their own. It's been a feedback loop. If you're going to have fights around the world, you have to have fighters from around the world. So as UFC becomes global, I'm stepping foot in places I never thought I'd see. Over the past 14 years, the infrastructure for UFC has been built up around the globe. It's fitting, I think, since many of the disciplines that the fighters practice, from judo to jiu-jitsu to taekwondo, originated in foreign places.

I think of Zhang Weili walking out to a Chinese song and waving a Chinese flag, Joanna Jędrzejczyk from Poland, Conor Mcgregor from Ireland, Anderson Silva from Brazil and Khabib Nurmagomedov from Dagestan. I picture Roman Dolidze, a fighter from the small Eastern European country of Georgia screaming out in joy, in his language, after a victory. I didn't know what he was saying, neither did most fans, but that didn't matter. We all understood.

Dana has always said that if you have a four-cornered street anywhere in the world, with a basketball game, a tennis match, a soccer match, and a fight happening at once, the fight will always draw the crowd. It's a visceral reaction; people want to see it. They will drop what they're doing to go see it. There's no learning curve to understanding how a fight works. UFC can go to countries who know nothing about American sports, but they all know the basics of what we're doing. Even if you don't speak the language, share the culture, or understand the technical aspects, you can still appreciate the excitement and athleticism. Neither professional football, nor baseball translate in the same way. UFC is unique in that regard.

When UFC comes to town, it is now front-page news, enveloping the area, bringing the locals together like a circus. I feel proud that I've been part of a team that has helped to spread it. MMA is now mainstream: kids have their favorite fighters, take classes in the suburbs, and get together on a Saturday night to watch a fight—just as my generation did for boxing. The sport continues to expand into a huge untapped audience in Eastern Europe, and UFC has opened a UFC Performance Institute in Shanghai, three times larger than the one in Las Vegas. It should help develop fighters there, bringing the sport truly worldwide.

The technology also moves forward. We've had discussions of developing MMA gloves with data sensors that can measure the velocity of each punch. Soon, fans will be able to see on their television what the punch was and whether it landed in a scoring area, similar to what's happened with baseball pitching in recent years. There are discussions of putting in a sensor in the mouthpiece that'll measure velocity, too. Eventually, analytics will come into play on a level we can't even conceive of, but we're ready for it. There are writers and fans who want "open scoring" where the judges' scores for each round are broadcast as they happen. I'm against it. I would hate to lose the surprising impact of one of the most iconic moments in all of sports when Bruce Buffer says "And new…" or "And still…" Some things are better the way they are.

Speaking of surprises, November 2020 brought an unforgettable moment in my life, during one of the most unprecedented years I've ever experienced in my career. The COVID-19 pandemic had affected nearly everyone and everything on the globe for most of the year, but the UFC organization still managed to put on safe, entertaining events almost every week. Sitting Octagonside at the UFC APEX in Las Vegas during the main card of UFC 255 waiting for a pair of championship fights to start, I was announced as an inductee into the 2020 class of the UFC Hall of Fame, recognizing my contributions to the sport of mixed martial arts. To say this incredible honor was overwhelming is putting it lightly, as I had completely no idea it was coming. It was even more wonderful to see my wife and children step out from behind the curtain in the arena to share this special moment with, along with Dana, UFC staff and members of the press with whom I'd shared so many memories throughout the years.

Las Vegas is a strange place to grow up, but I've been here so long. It's the only home I know. I don't live on the Strip or in a hotel or near the stadiums, but I do come to work there. I like spending some of my week in that world, the performance world, the entertainment capital of America. There's really nowhere else like it.

Sports in Las Vegas once only meant gambling and boxing, but now it's like any major city. We have an NHL hockey team with the Golden Knights and an NFL team with the Raiders, and a WNBA team with the Aces. One day, the NBA will come, too. I think it's inevitable.

Major music stars do residencies at the hotels, and with the opening of Allegiant Stadium, other leading musical acts will come as well. We have kid-friendly activities all over town, celebrity chefs setting up restaurants, and major retailers with stores on the Strip and beyond. It's a different world from the one I arrived to in the late 1950s—even a different world from the one in the 1980s when I first began to work in boxing.

Some things remain, though. The anticipation in the air on fight night, the roar of the crowd, the buzz you get seeing fighters under the bright lights. I still run the shot clock at UNLV basketball games, and I am still the commissioner of officials for high school sports. I like that connection, to my own past, to the community, and to the sports world. It's why I have officiated for so long and continued to long into my professional boxing career. It's why I'll be at Raiders' home games every week as their Player to Coach Communications Operator, cutting off the quarterbacks' and defensive signal callers' headsets at the 15-second mark on the play clock. I get a rush from being, well not exactly *on* the field, but inside the game. I always have.

You can never plan for where you'll end up. I think back to that advertisement about football referees that first set me on this path, and it just blows my mind, where it all led. *What a long, strange trip it has been*, indeed.

But I'm not done yet.

End Notes

■ ■ ■

1. **The sweet science:** Quoted in David Remnick, "Reporting It All," New Yorker, March 22, 2004
2. **The thrill of heavyweights:** Thomas Hauser, "Not all fights have to be for a title," ESPN.com, October 9, 2007
3. **It also produced:** Kimball "Disarming Candor," *At the Fights*, xii in
4. **In the words one writer:** Jonathan Snowden, "How Las Vegas Became the Boxing Capital of the World, Bleacher Report, September 11, 2014
5. **Boxing writer A.J.:** Liebling, "Poet and Pedagogue," *A Neutral Corner*, 163
6. **After taking in the match:** David Remnick, *King of the World: Muhammad Ali and the Rise of an American Hero* (New York: Random House, 1998) 120
7. **From then on, Clay:** Randy Roberts and Johnny Smith, "The Branding of Muhammad Ali," The New Republic, June 4, 2016
8. **"old fashioned murder":** John P. Carmichael quoted in Liebling, *A Neutral Corner 183*
9. **"the first intimidating fighter":** Tyson is quoted in film "Pariah: The Lives and Deaths of Sonny Liston" (dir. Simon George), 2019

[10] **The best that ever:** Tim Dahlberg, *Fight Town: Las Vegas – The Boxing Capital of The World*, (Las Vegas: Stephens Press, 2007)

[11] **"the last golden age":** George Kimball, *Four Kings: Leonard, Hagler, Hearns, Duran and the Last Great Era of Boxing* (New York: McBooks Press, 2008) ix

[12] **Those four had nine:** Kimball, xvii

[13] **If a boxing match:** Joyce Carol Oates, *On Boxing* (New York: Doubleday, 1987)

[14] **"Think of King as":** Kimball, 67

[15] **Arum promoted the match:** Thomas Hauser, *Boxing Is…Reflections on the Sweet Science* (Fayetteville: University of Arkansas Press, 2010) 125

[16] **"having mastered a new language":** Kimball, 64

[17] **"a snake in the grass":** *At the Fights: American Writers on Boxing: A Library of America Special Publication* (Washington, D.C.: Library of America, 2012)

[18] **"the blood and bones:** Katherine Dunn, *One Ring Circus: Dispatches from the World of Boxing* (Tucson: Schaffner Press, 2009)

[19] **Hunger and pride:** Jerry Izenberg, *Once There Were Giants* (New York: Skyhorse, 2017)

[20] **"Everyone knew who he":** Hauser, *Boxing is…*, 171

[21] **"Most guys lost the fight":** *Tyson* (dir. James Toback), 2008

[22] **"lacked the killer instinct":** Remnick, *King of the World*, 13

[23] **"like a man trying to cross":** Izenberg

[24] **They would've doubled:** "The Champ," Readers Digest, 1/72, 109

[25] **Boxers were liars:** Norman Mailer, *The Fight* (New York: Random House, 1975) 43

[26] **"It's easy to do anything":** Gay Talese, "The Loser," *Esquire*, March 1964

[27] **When boxing falls short:** Dunn, ix

[28] **De La Hoya was a:** Thomas Hauser, *The Boxing Scene*, (Philadelphia: Temple University Press, 2009) 17

[29] **"When I was little":** Thomas Hauser, "De La Hoya- Mayweather in

Perspective," The Boxing Scene (Philadelphia: Temple University Press, 2009), 24

30 **At first, the referee:** Marissa Payne, "UFC's climb, 23 years to the day, from 'freak show' to one of sport's most sacred stages" *Washington Post,* November 10, 2016.

31 **"Most people have never":** Hauser, *The Boxing Scene,* 151

32 **"built like a granite:"** Daniel Van Boom, "Meet Robert Whittaker, the UFC champ who uses Microsoft Excel to smash opponents," CNET, February 8, 2019 Daniel Van Boom, "Meet Robert Whittaker, the UFC champ who uses Microsoft Excel to smash opponents," CNET, February 8, 2019

33 **"a celebration all around":** Simon Head, "Is UFC one of the most progressive LGBTQ+ friendly sports?" BBC, May 10, 2018

Printed in Great Britain
by Amazon